Lifting the Darkness

Thirty years on the road with Tough Talk

**By Arthur White and Ian McDowall
with Jude Simpson**

Authentic

31 30 29 28 27 26 25   7 6 5 4 3 2 1

First published 2025 by Authentic Media Limited,
PO Box 6326, Bletchley, Milton Keynes, MK1 9GG.
authenticmedia.co.uk

British Library Cataloguing in Publication Data
A catalogue record for this book is available from the British Library.
ISBN: 978-1-78893-380-3
978-1- 78893-381-0 (e-book)

Scripture quotations marked ERV are taken from the
HOLY BIBLE: EASY-TO-READ VERSION
© 2014 by Bible League International. Used by permission.

Scripture quotations marked KJV are from The Authorized (King James) Version.
Rights in the Authorized Version in the United Kingdom are vested in the Crown.
Reproduced by permission of the Crown's patentee, Cambridge University Press.

Scripture quotations marked NIV are taken from
The Holy Bible, New International Version Anglicised
Copyright © 1979, 1984, 2011 Biblica
Used by permission of Hodder & Stoughton Ltd, an Hachette UK company.
All rights reserved. 'NIV' is a registered trademark of Biblica UK trademark number 1448790.

Scripture quotations marked NKJV taken from the New King James Version®.
Copyright © 1982 by Thomas Nelson. Used by permission. All rights reserved.

Scripture quotations marked NLV are taken from the *New Life Version*,
Copyright © 1969 and 2003.
Used by permission of Barbour Publishing, Inc., Uhrichsville, Ohio 44683.
All rights reserved.

Cover design by David Lund

Printed and bound by CPI Group (UK) Ltd, Croydon, CR0 4YY

Some of the names and identifying details have been changed in this book for anonymity.

This book is dedicated to everyone
who has supported Tough Talk
over the last thirty years

Contents

Foreword

A number of years ago, I was sitting in a small front room with two hard-looking men. One had been a detective in what was once known as the Royal Ulster Constabulary. The other had been a member of the Provisional IRA. They were sitting there, chatting away like old mates eating tea cakes. I was somewhat perplexed.

'How has this friendship come about?' I asked them.

One of them looked up from his tea cake and stared at me directly with a hint of a smile and a tinge of warmth around his eyes.

'Well we used to hunt each other on the streets of Belfast, but then we both met Jesus and now we are on the men's breakfast planning committee.'

Only Jesus.

Only Jesus can turn hard, violent men who were sworn enemies into tea cake-sharing buddies.

No self-help book, no counselling or therapy can transform lives like the message of Jesus Christ.

That's where Tough Talk come in.

I first met them in 1998, although Arthur White (now one of my closest mates) doesn't remember. Something I occasionally pull out and rib him about.

I was planting a church on a tough Essex estate as a young 20-something. A few months earlier I had gone to what was called, 'The Christian Resources Exhibition'. It's really not my cup of tea, but the church needed some resources and I had been dispatched against my will.

As I ambled among the Christian sock sellers, the alternative bells, clerical robe stands and so on I was feeling my life force drain away from me. Now I've nothing against these things, each to their own I say, I just detest shopping and I don't really like crowded aisles.

Then I heard this booming voice. Essex accent like me. Straight talking, no nonsense, no jargon. It sounded like a gnarly gangster telling everyone that Jesus gets all the glory. I followed the voice and stumbled upon an awards presentation where a group called Tough Talk were getting some accolade or other. Not that they seemed bothered about that in the slightest. They were trying to tell everyone about Jesus just in case someone there wasn't a believer.

I loved it! Actually I was mesmerised. This was more like it!

In that moment I felt a renewed energy to give it large for Jesus. They were so inspiring. I also decided in that moment I would see if I could get them to my little church to do some mission stuff. I had no clue how we would afford it. I was unpaid myself and burning through my savings trying to pioneer a church in a very poor estate. In those contexts you don't get much in the way of offerings you see.

The rest, for me, is history. These men were the real deal. They weren't bothered about money. They just wanted to get in front of people and talk about Jesus. They came, they blew the doors off and many came to know Jesus.

So who are they? Well, they are 'unschooled ordinary men' who have met Jesus.

They don't glorify their pasts. They are variously from the occult, violent crime, door keeping and so on. Living on their wits, armed and accustomed to violence and confrontation, some of them were once very dangerous men. In addition, Ian McDowall had been a body builder, while Joe Lampshire and others had been power lifters. One of them (Arthur White) was a multiple record holder and world champion.

Then each of them met Jesus.

So powerful were their transformations that they could do nothing but share what they had found. To this day they haven't stopped. From military bases to the toughest prisons, from church fetes to small working men's clubs to some of the biggest platforms going. They will go wherever they can to share Christ. Ferociously biblical, as bold as they come. Standing on street corners or in a café, they are the same.

It's a privilege to call them friends. They inspire me to this day and I know this book will inspire you and compel you to look to Christ and/or be renewed in your confidence in the gospel in a powerful way.

Thank you Tough Talk. There are many more chapters yet to come.

Carl Beech
President of Christian Vision for Men (CVM),
founder of 'The Gathering', CEO of Edge Ministries and
voluntary CEO of Spotlight YOPD – the
young onset Parkinson's charity

Chapter One

''Ello, Son, My Name's Arfa!'

And He said to them, 'Go into all the world and preach the
gospel to every creature.'

Mark 16:15, NKJV

Arthur

If you hear me speak, you'll know from my less-than-delicate
tones that I wasn't educated at Cambridge. I come straight out
of the East End of London. I was one of four kids brought up
on a council estate, in an ordinary working-class family.

There was certainly no money in my family. I didn't have
a bad life, though. I was pretty good at sport, and that's all I
really wanted to do. I remember watching Bobby Charlton
playing in the World Cup in 1966, and I was thinking, 'that's
where I wanna be – kicking a football, scoring a goal, winning.'

I took part in every single sport I could, and I started training in the gym when I was in my mid-teens. I loved life and I
had a good life.

I met my wife aged 14. We got engaged at 17, and married at 19. I've now got two grown-up children and three

grandchildren. We've been married for about fifty-four years. When I'm telling my story, I always get applause at that point. Not always when I say I was a world champion, or even a world record holder. But when I say I've been married fifty-four years, they always applaud!

I had a good life. I left school with no academic qualifications, but I served an apprenticeship as a carpenter. Then, when I finished my apprenticeship, I started to work for myself and I built up my own business. I was in the building trade. In the mid-1980s I was turning over a few million quid, I had fifty men working for me and 250 subcontractors running around. I was doing good for a kid off the estate. I was also a powerlifter.

Powerlifting is different to weightlifting. To compete in weightlifting, you perform two different overhead lifts; the snatch, and the clean-and-jerk. In powerlifting, you compete in three lifts; the squat, the bench press and the deadlift. At my peak, I was deadlifting 380kg. That's about the weight of four and a half British men.

I was a powerlifter. Ian was a bodybuilder. Joe was a powerlifter.

Ian

It hadn't quite dawned on me that Arthur was a powerlifter. It was 1995 when we first met each other. A guy called Frank Pratt had invited me to a men's breakfast in London, run by the Full Gospel Business men's fellowship (FGB).

I was sitting there, and to be honest I felt a bit like a fish out of water. I'm not the most sociable individual, and I didn't know anyone. There were 200 or 300 men at this breakfast event, and the only empty seat was next to mine. It was like no one wanted to sit next to me.

Then this bloke bowled in, and said, in a proper East End accent, 'Is this seat free, then?'

I nodded. 'Yeah, it is, mate.'

I must have been in my late twenties, and this guy was in his forties. He sat down and said – again, in that Cockney twang, "Ello, son. My name's Arfa!'

I introduced myself, we started talking, and it turned out we had a bit in common. We'd both been invited there by Frank Pratt, we both lived in Essex, and I remember Arthur looking at me and saying, 'You look like you've done a bit of weightlifting, boy.'

At the time, I think Arthur had a dodgy knee, and had been on some kind of fast, so he didn't look like a powerlifter, and I didn't particularly want to open up about weights or training. I just went, 'Yeah, I've done a bit, mate.'

But as we talked, my ears pricked up more and more, because he told me his testimony. He told me what his life had been like, and how he'd met God and become a Christian and everything had turned around. I remember getting his details, and I invited him to come to a prison with me.

Arthur

Back in the 1980s, I had – materialistically speaking – everything you would want in life. Yet I was never, ever content. I wanted more contracts, a bigger house, a better car. I'd sometimes go out to work in a Jaguar, and come back home in a Mercedes. My wife used to go ballistic! But I loved those posh cars. I was hankering after a Rolls-Royce. I saw a lovely one – chocolate brown, cream upholstery with dark-brown piping. I was desperate to get that Roller, but someone else bought it before me.

It was the same in my sport. Every time I competed, I wanted another record. I had a thirty-year powerlifting career, during which I won nine British titles, six European titles and four world titles between 1976 and 2006. I was in the Guinness book of records in 1987, and initiated into the powerlifting 'Hall of Fame' in 1989. But all that time, all I wanted was more. My wife would say, 'When are you ever going to be content?'

Having drive and ambition is a good thing. Nothing wrong with it. I've got an ambition now. I want to be in Glory with the Lord! But back then, my drive, ambition and discontent were causing me a problem. I was searching and searching, and never finding.

I'd never smoked – I'd never seen the attraction – and I hardly drank at all. I certainly never took drugs. I was clean as a young man, and I was proud of that. But slowly, bit by bit, I started taking a little bit of this and that. It was just to help my performance, help me rest and build muscle, but it spiralled. I got to the point where I was addicted to steroids and to cocaine. I was injecting myself with steroids. I was putting cocaine on my cornflakes for breakfast, and in my coffee.

I was driving on, pushing on, spending more and more time in the gym, more and more obsessed with my lifting. My drug addiction was ruining my life. It was eating up my income. Not only was it changing me physically, it was starting to change the way I thought as well.

I had an affair with a young woman. It was stupid. I left my wife, and I deserted my children. Then I lost my business.

I was spending more and more time in the gym, and the guys who worked for me realised this, so as soon as I left the building site to go to the gym, they left as well, and the work didn't get done. I lost my business, my homes, my wife, my money. My wife has calculated that I spent and wasted about a million pounds. Everything I ever worked for I lost in four years of madness. I lost the respect of other people, and eventually I lost my own self-respect as well.

I developed pains in my chest in 1992 after a World Championship competition that I won. I went to see a doctor who was a friend of mine, and he said, 'Arthur, you've got to stop taking these drugs.' He knew what I was on – I was quite open about it. He said, 'Your heart's racing like a Formula One car, it can't take the pressure.' My heart had ballooned to the size of a small football.

So, the drugs were taking a toll on me. My mental health issues were escalating. I was suffering bouts of severe depression. I was in a pit.

I won the world title, and the European title on the same day. I won Best Lifter in Europe and second best in the world. I broke sixteen British, European, Commonwealth and world records that very day. It was the pinnacle of my lifting career, and the pinnacle of my physical condition – externally. But internally, my head was smashed, and that very evening, I tried to cut my own throat. I wanted to end my life, because I could see no way out.

Ian

When I had recently become a Christian, I remember sitting in church, thinking, 'What the heck do I do now?' This would have been around 1993 or 1994. I had stopped a load of things that I had been doing in life, because I knew they weren't right. I was no longer carrying weapons. I was stopping all the fighting. It was all changing. But what to put in its place?

I was looking round the church at everyone else, thinking, 'I've become a Christian, but I can't dance or sing. I'm not a pastor, or a worship leader. I'm not even good at making coffee for people. What do Christians like me do?'

I was still working as a doorman at this point, and I was sharing my story with the guys I was working with – telling them how God had changed my life. I was bringing other doormen to church, because they wanted to know more. So people started saying to me, 'You're an evangelist, Ian. You're evangelising.'

I remember going to listen to a guy called Barry Smith. I think it was at Shooter's Hill in south-east London. He was a crazy, big evangelist character, who talked a lot about the end of the world and heaven and hell, and I loved him. He was a great speaker; he was so funny and his stories were so dramatic and compelling. I remember him saying,

'I wanted to tell people about Jesus, so I started putting posters up that said, "*Come and hear stories about the end of the world*".' That's how he had started. I remember storing that little bit of information away in my head.

I was going to church in Ilford, and a guy called Steve Derbyshire was my pastor. A number of these doormen and bouncers I was bringing to church were themselves believing in Jesus and coming to faith, and one day Steve said to me, 'Ian, why don't you bring your weights and a few of your guys one evening? You can lift the weights, and share some testimonies, and we'll see what happens.'

Years later, Steve told me he really wanted to do some outreach at his church, but had no budget to pay for people to come in and run the event, so asking me was his way of getting it done! But if the format of Tough Talk started anywhere, it was there with Steve Derbyshire, with a group of men who talked about their experience of God, and showed people what powerlifting looked like. For me, I didn't really care about lifting the weights, I just wanted to get the stories told, and the gospel preached. But Steve said, 'Bring your weights as well.'

Steve got some posters done, which we put up, and they said, *'Come and see some powerlifters!'*

Now, I and the other guys at that point, actually, we were much more into bodybuilding than powerlifting. I had started lifting weights around the age of 13, and begun my bodybuilding career aged 16 or 17, winning a large number of county and British trophies.

Anyway, that didn't matter too much to me. There's a bit of a crossover in the sense that you do the same kind of training in the gym for both those disciplines, and besides, I wasn't convinced at this point that the weights were going to connect with anyone. In fact, I wasn't convinced that any of the stories would connect with people, either. But I kind of thought, 'Let's give it a go, as a one-off.'

We were a pretty intimidating collection of guys back then – scary fellas, to be honest. Some of the guys in the room were pretty dangerous characters – massive lumps of men who would come to the microphone with big, gravelly voices to talk about their faith.

We'd only been Christians a few months – we weren't mature Christians at all. But there were some incredible stories, really supernatural stories from these guys, about being rescued from really dark, evil lives, and being brought into a place of peace and light with God.

So we lifted the weights, and we told our stories, and then Steve Derbyshire made an appeal – he told people that we are all lost in God's eyes, but that God wants to forgive us our sins, and get back in charge of our lives, and that he's made that possible through the death of the man Jesus, who was also God, who paid the price that we should have paid for the mess we've made of life. He invited people to come to the front if they wanted to believe that day, and four or five people came forward to receive Jesus Christ.

I was surprised, to be honest. I hadn't expected that. I was amazed, really, that people had listened to us, watched us, and that the Holy Spirit had then done something in their heads that made them want to respond to Christ.

So, I thought to myself, right, what next?

Arthur

I tried to take my own life on a number of occasions. I tried cutting my own throat. I tried crashing the car. I tried taking an overdose, I even tried to drown myself in Tenerife. I saw no way out. The doctor was telling me I was killing myself anyway, with the drugs.

Having lost my business, I started working as a bouncer, and as a debt collector. This was not the sort of debt collecting that is governed by the Office of Fair Trading. You wouldn't get a polite letter from me giving you seven days to pay up. If I knew where you lived, I'd come round, kick the door in, drag you out, bash you up and try to get a few quid out of you. It was a risky business, but I needed the money for the drugs.

I was making a lot of enemies, and in my neck of the woods, there were plenty of guys who would be more than capable of finishing me off if they wanted to, and probably wouldn't think twice about it. So, when I went out, I had a 12-inch diver's knife strapped to one arm, a .38 Beretta in the other pocket, two knuckledusters always on me, two club hammers under the seat of my car, and a pickaxe handle in my boot.

That's where I'd got to. From that sporty kid who just wanted to be like Bobby Charlton, here I was tearing round the East End of London, fighting almost every day.

I was a violent man, and my life was constantly on a knife edge. I knew something had to change. I was living apart from my wife, but at one point she had given me the name of a counsellor, saying, 'You need to sort yourself out.'

I'd resisted. I'd rejected the idea. But it got to the point where I started to realise I couldn't sort things out myself. So, I went to see this counsellor. I just thought maybe he could help me. I didn't know till I got there that this guy was a Christian.

I actually took my knife off my arm before I went in, because I didn't want him to see I was carrying that – it didn't seem very respectable. I strapped it down my boot instead.

This Christian man said something to me that has always stuck with me. He said, 'You need to choose. Arthur, there are consequences to your actions.' Well, that made sense – the consequence of my actions was that my life was close to ending. 'And *you* need to make a choice.'

Now, at that point in my life, I could barely choose which shirt to put on in the morning, let alone choose how to change my life, but that night, after my debt collecting, I pulled up in the car park in Spitalfields fruit and veg market, and I got out and stood there in the cold. I was on my own. No background music. No one egging me on. Nothing. Just me.

And I cried out to God. I said, 'God, if you are there, if there is such a thing, come on then. Sort me out.'

Ian

After that first event, in our church with Steve Derbyshire, I started hiring out venues – in Clacton, Southend, Chingford – a leisure centre here, a boxing club there. I remembered Barry Smith, and the way he'd started just with some posters (this was way before the internet, mobile phones or social media), so we put posters and fliers up everywhere. And when I say everywhere, I mean, everywhere! At one point, we flooded Clacton with 50,000 fliers! I got two of my younger brothers to help me, and we got in trouble with the council for it. We'd plastered them in newspapers, on doors, all over the walls, everywhere. They all said, '*Come and hear stories from East End hardmen!*'

And they had the time, date, venue and a phone number, of course.

I got a call from the local council, and they were furious. 'Your fliers are all over the place. You can't do that, it's illegal,' they said. 'You've got to remove these posters as soon as possible, or we'll close down your event!'

I blagged it on the phone. I apologised nicely and sounded surprised: 'Apologies, mate. Sorry about that. I had no idea they were put up like that. I'll have a word with the young guy I asked to distribute them for me. Don't worry, we'll get it sorted.' Of course, I'd told them to plaster the fliers all over the place, and I'd done a load of them myself as well. We'd got pretty enthusiastic about it. Now I had to get them all taken down again! I got my brother and his mates to run around taking down all the fliers, so the council wouldn't close us down. But actually, the events all went well. People came, people listened, people were interested. And some people responded. Plus, every event we did, we got more bookings off the back of it.

We did more and more events. We made tapes of our testimonies, because people wanted to hear them, and we started giving them out at the end of the events. It was a groundswell – we did the stuff, people booked us, we did the stuff again, more people booked us – we were doing churches, gyms, halls, whatever. It wasn't very organised but it was pretty exciting.

I started running a Tuesday night prayer meeting in my office for the guys who were involved, to pray for each other and pray for the events. I knew from the start that we had to depend on God, and on the presence and involvement of the Holy Spirit.

Then, around March 1996, there was a church in Wood Green – The Powerhouse, it was called. The pastor was young and dynamic, and he booked us for an event. He wanted to take some pictures of us in the gym for the publicity. So, we went down the gym, and he took some photos, and he made this poster, for his event. The poster said: '*Tough Talk: Come and hear incredible stories from hardmen, and watch some powerlifting!*' On the poster were some of the photos he'd taken – us guys in our gym kit, doing bicep curls. I barely noticed that he'd used this phrase 'Tough Talk' because I was too busy cringing at the bicep curls. Bicep curls have nothing to do with powerlifting! It's like having a picture of someone doing karate to advertise a boxing match, or a juggler to advertise a game of basketball. In fact, I remember Arthur picking up that poster in my office one time, when he came to a prayer meeting, and just laughing at the bicep curls.

Arthur

I love a challenge. I still love a challenge. I don't want to get old. I don't want my grandkids to say, 'He's a lovely old man', I want them to say, '*What* is Grandad up to now? What *on earth* is he doing!'

Even now, at the age of 73, when my wife comes out to the garage, I've got the *Rocky*[1] music on and I'm lifting the weights. These days I'm sitting down to lift them, but I'm doing it, nonetheless.

That night in Spitalfields Market car park, I chose to ask God to come into my life. There was no booming voice, no choir of angels and the heavens didn't open. But for the first time in my life, I remember looking into the darkness, and I wasn't afraid. All my life, including all my adult life, I'd been afraid of the dark. Yet it was as if scales had been lifted off my eyes. It was pitch black where I'd parked my van up. It was dark as anything. But I was looking across the car park and I wasn't afraid. I could see a light.

My drug addiction stopped that night. I started going to church. I started reading my Bible. I started to pray. My life started to change. From the moment I cried out to God, from the moment I chose to turn away from the life I was living and put my trust in Jesus Christ, my life started to turn around.

I remember saying to God, 'Take this drug addiction away from me!' and he said, 'No, Arthur. You stop it. And I'll give you the strength to get through it.' And he did.

I would wake up many nights during that process, shaking, sweating, with fear pouring over me, falling out of the bed and writhing on the floor. I believed the devil was having a pop at me, attacking me, and each time, I cried out to Jesus. I remember many times, literally crying out, '*Jesus*! Put me to sleep!' And the next thing I knew, I'd be waking up in the morning. I was still on the floor, but I'd been asleep and I woke up refreshed, and I wasn't taking the drugs any more.

My wife and I were apart for four years. We got remarried in 1993. We've been back together more than thirty years now. And in that whole thirty years, she's never thrown it in my face, what I did to her. She knows I'm sorry and she knows I've changed, and she's an incredibly gracious woman.

So, having thrown everything away, I got everything back again – everything that matters. Now, I have the love and respect of my wife. I have the love and respect of my children. Most of all, I have the love and forgiveness of Jesus Christ, my Saviour, the Prince of Peace. I have everything I need in life. In the Bible, Peter writes, 'His divine power has given us everything we need for a godly life' (2 Pet. 1:3, NIV) and that is truly my experience. If my life ends today – Ian always tells me this had better not happen in his van, on the way home from an event – but if it does, I know where I'm going. If God calls me I'm going to be in Glory with him.

In the meantime, I'm certain of three things: forgiveness of my past, peace in the present and hope for the future.

While he puts breath in my lungs, I will stand up and testify to Jesus Christ. While Joe and Ian get me round the country, into prisons and schools, up on stages and platforms, into gyms and scout huts and street corners, I'll testify to Jesus Christ. I will boast only in Jesus Christ, and in his cross, because it's Jesus who set me free.

Ian

By the time I met Arthur at the FGB breakfast, up in central London, I was doing all these events, with various guys, in various places. I'd been through some ups and downs, but it was growing and it was pretty exciting.

I said to Arthur,

'Come along to a prison with me.'

I was regularly going into Highpoint prison, which was the first prison to invite me, around 1994 or so. I was taking some of the guys, and the weights, and telling our stories. I didn't care how I did it, I just wanted to evangelise. I wanted to tell people about Jesus Christ, who changes lives. It didn't matter how. Weights, doormen, prisons, chaplains, whatever. I just wanted any opportunity to preach the gospel. And I thought, 'Arthur's might be a good testimony to tell at the prison.'

So, we met up in Loughton, and I took Arthur to this prison with me, and he gave a bit of testimony. It still hadn't dawned on me that Arthur was this world-class powerlifter! I even heard his story, and he did mention the powerlifting, but I wasn't focused on that. For me, it was all about the dramatic life change. Arthur, like me, had been a violent man, a hardman, a gangster. At the time, I had characters around me that had been Mafia gangsters and doormen, terrorists and hitmen and everything, and so my real focus was all about the hardcore stories, and how Jesus Christ could change even the hardest, most violent heart.

Arthur started coming to more events with us; his testimony was powerful, and because he was a really engaging speaker, I wasn't really using him much to actually lift the weights!

About a year after meeting Arf – sometime in 1997 – I was invited back to my own church in Ilford again. The pastor, Steve said, 'This is great! You're doing all this stuff. It's going so well, and you're going far and wide. Come back and do a session for us again.'

So, he set up an event, and he also called it 'Tough Talk', and this time I thought to myself, 'That's a good name for it.' Then I was listening to Arthur giving his testimony there, and I realised properly, for the first time, that he was a powerlifter. Not only was he an actual powerlifter (the rest of us were bodybuilders who used powerlifting exercises for training) but he was a world champion powerlifter – four times over! And that's when it hit me.

I thought, 'This is what we do! We demonstrate powerlifting, which is the hook that draws people in. Then we tell our stories – of violent lives that have been totally changed through faith – and after that, we preach the gospel of Jesus Christ. We tell people that Jesus is powerful to forgive sins and change lives, and we invite them to respond.

'That's it,' I thought. 'That's the ministry. And it's called Tough Talk.'

He said to them, 'Go everywhere in the world. Tell the Good News to everyone.'

Mark 16:15, ERV

Chapter Two

Behind Bars

> I was naked and you clothed Me; I was sick and you visited
> Me; I was in prison and you came to Me.
>
> *Matt. 25:36, NKJV*

Ian

HMP Highpoint in Suffolk was one of the first prisons I spoke in – right at the start, when the ministry was only just getting going. I was invited by the chaplain. I just went in by myself, and told my story about coming to Jesus from a background of drug abuse, violence and aggression. I told my story, and I told them the gospel.

Straight away, the guys were listening and engaged. In fact, we've always found that our events have a powerful and immediate impact on prisoners. Guys in prison have lost hope. They often don't even believe they have a choice. They feel hard done by, or they feel self-loathing, or both. When we tell our stories, there's a lot for them to relate to.

I started taking other guys into prisons with me, and we would also take the weights – which were a big draw. There's not a lot to do in prisons, and one thing they like to spend time on is training. They are interested in building muscle, fitness and strength. They also like to be in decent physical condition because of status in the prison – making sure of your place in the pecking order.

When chaplains contacted us to book Tough Talk for prison events, we started suggesting that they also mention it to the gym staff, as we realised that would work as well – and would reach the prisoners who didn't come to chapel. So, we started doing some of our events in the chapel, and some in the gym – often both in the same prison.

Naturally, when we went into the gyms it felt like a different invitation and agenda, so we talked a bit more about our training, our careers and the steroid abuse. Every prison has a drugs issue, so the staff liked it when we came in and talked about steroids – which are one of the most popular drugs in prisons. But we always gave the gospel as well – it was just a different sort of balance compared to the meetings in chapels.

HMP/YOI Feltham was one of the prisons where they really responded to the weights. Feltham is a Young Offenders Institution (YOI), so it's full of young people aged between 15 and 21, some on remand, some convicted. It was a violent, troublesome sort of place, where you felt something might kick off at any minute. I remember being in there once, at the end of an event, when a fight broke out between two of the prisoners. Quick as a flash they were down on the floor, rolling around, and I remember I was chatting to a couple of other lads, and these two scrapping youngsters rolled towards us, towards the PA kit we had brought along. I remember just lifting up the speaker so they could roll right on under it, then putting it back down again when they'd gone through, and carrying on talking to these other young lads while the prison officers went to break up the fight.

At first, when we would arrive, the lads were often really circumspect. They looked afraid, or resistant, and suspicious of us. But as soon as we got out the weights, that suspicion would melt away. They connected with the lifting, and that made them listen to what we had to say. By the end, they'd be all over us like flies! Everybody wanted a Bible, wanted one of our books, wanted us to sign it for them, had a question to ask – and that switch often came when we got out the weights and started lifting.

Arthur

A lot of men would start their sentence in Feltham, then get transferred somewhere else when they were convicted, or as they got older. We had a great relationship with the chaplain, and there was a period in Tough Talk's early days when we were going in pretty much every month. So, we got to sow into a lot of young lives. Ever since that, many times, we've met a man in another prison, who has said, 'I saw you at Feltham, years ago!'

We did an event once at a church called Holy Trinity Brompton in London, and three men came up to us afterwards who were ex-prisoners and had seen us when they were inside. It was a bit embarrassing, in fact. One of them looked at us like we were celebrities. He said, 'I've just read your book . . . and now you're here!' He'd read our book when he was on remand in Pentonville Prison, and now he was out and coming to church. Another of the men had seen us ten or twelve years before. He was now working for a coffee business that employs a lot of ex-offenders. He was training to become a barista. The third guy had seen us twenty or twenty-five years ago, in prison, and had become a Christian. Our visit had been part of that.

We can see how many people visibly respond when we give an appeal at the end of our presentation, but we don't know what happens after that. So, it's brilliant when we meet these people and find out that God used us to affect their life very significantly, sometimes many years ago.

It's not a nice life, being in prison, and there's a spiritual battle going on, as well as the physical realities. When we went to Barlinnie prison, in Glasgow, only twenty or so years ago, they were still slopping out. It was a massive old Victorian building, which has now been decommissioned. The chapel there is huge – a dark, arched stone building, massive and very cold! It's a listed building. It probably held around a thousand men, and they all had to go to chapel each Sunday back then – it was compulsory.

On that first occasion, we took our own PA – the first set we had – but it was a total disaster with the acoustics under that massive, vaulted ceiling. We ended up just switching it off and yelling instead.

We lifted the weights there in the chapel, and we did a bench press competition for the prisoners – it's a great way to get them involved. Then we told our stories, and we preached the gospel. We made an altar call – we said, 'If you want to make a choice today, to turn away from the things that are wrong in your life, and turn to Christ, who wants to save you, then stick your hand up.' A lot of men raised their hands.

Ian

Afterwards we came out, and there were heaps of family members queueing up to visit the prisoners. We had a lad with us, and he was carrying the PA – it was a big, hulking old speaker, and he was doing a bit of a macho job, trying to show that he could manage it easily.

There was a lawn all around the front of the prison, which sloped downwards, and had some steps in it. But the steps were crowded with family members queueing to get in, so for some reason, despite the cold, wet Scottish weather, this lad decided to avoid the crowded steps and carry the heavy PA straight down the grassy slope.

Inevitably, he slipped, then skidded, fell over and slid on his back right down the slope, still hugging this massive speaker, like some kind of human tortoise. The queue of people stared, then laughed, then ended up cheering as he struggled back to his feet, caked in mud.

Arf and I kept our heads down at that point!

Arthur

Once when we went into a prison, the chaplain told us about a previous team of evangelists who had gone in, who had caused havoc. They'd strode in there and got straight on preaching heaven and hell, and people were walking out, shouting at them. There was no relationship.

We believe in heaven and hell, but we've always asked the Holy Spirit to give us wisdom, to keep doors open and to give us the ability to connect. We want to preach the gospel – and that isn't going to happen if we burn all our bridges.

We always tell people from the start who we are. We say, 'We are Tough Talk. We're a registered Christian charity. We've been invited here by the chaplain. We haven't come to big ourselves up, to patronise you, or to talk down to you. We've come here to share with you something about our lives. A lot of what we're going to say we're actually ashamed of. We will have some fun lifting the weights, but we want to share with you what we consider is the most important thing in our lives, and that is our faith and our trust in Jesus Christ.'

Ian

When you look a man in the eye, they've got to know that you believe what you're saying you believe. In a warm, Christian environment, you feel sometimes like you could pull the wool over people's eyes – they would go along with whatever you're saying. But in a prison – and also in the Armed Forces, actually – there's no chance. From the moment you walk in, they're weighing you up. If they see anything false about you, you've lost them.

Arthur

Even in Young Offender prisons, the kids will weigh you up. It frightens the life out of me in some ways, because I've never been perfect, and I never will be, and sometimes you feel their eyes boring through you. I just keep making sure I've got a clear conscience before God, and a clear conscience before Ian and Joe. We keep each other on the straight and narrow, and that way we can be effective for God.

HMP Shotts in Scotland is another prison we've been to quite a few times. It has a very high security area – a bit like a prison-within-the-prison – where the most dangerous prisoners are housed . . . the ones who have committed the most heinous crimes. I remember the unit was horseshoe-shaped so the prison officers could always see what was going on from the middle.

We do a lot of work with disturbed men. We see a lot of evil. There is a good reason why these guys are in prison, and the evil is real. There's a battle going on before you even open your mouth.

There was a heavy, dark atmosphere in HMP Shotts. It was early in our ministry when I first went there, and I remember the threatening atmosphere well. There was much less of an obvious response to our presentation there, compared to other prisons. People weren't clamouring to put their hands up or come forward. But that doesn't mean nothing has happened.

We genuinely believe that there's another reality – the spiritual reality – that we can't see, but that is very powerful. There are forces who are opposed to the light of Jesus. There's a battle between good and evil. It's going on inside us all, and also around us, especially in places like Shotts.

Sometimes I think, if you could see what was happening in the spiritual reality, you would see things changing as we walked in. Spiritually, we would be kicking doors down. I believe that. When we go in, and speak our faith, I think God is breaking strongholds.

'"Not by strength nor by power, but by My Spirit," says the LORD' (Zech. 4:6, NLV). We go in very aware of our human weakness. But simply by speaking the truth of our lives, and the truth of the gospel, we are waging spiritual warfare. The enemy can't stand it.

Ian

In most prisons, the inmates will have duties or jobs as part of prison life. In Scottish prisons, there are gym orderlies, known as 'Pass Men' who are prisoners but also work in the gym. They wear sportswear, quite similar to the prison officers who work in the gym – so you can't always tell the difference straight away.

One time, I was showering and changing after the talk we'd given – I'd been lifting that day – and a guy came in, and we got chatting. I was half-naked, not finished dressing, and during the conversation, it dawned on me that this was a prisoner, not a guard. He was in for murder. It was just me and him in the room. And I only had my pants on.

He was asking me these spiritual questions, about God, and good and evil, and heaven and hell, and I remember trying to concentrate, give answers and make sense, but all I could think was that I was trapped in a changing room with a murderer, wearing nothing but my second-best Y-fronts. I just wanted to get my tracksuit on and get out of there!

Arthur

We usually go into prisons as a team, but we've both done quite a few prison visits on our own as well. The first prison I went to on my own as Tough Talk was Swaleside. It's a men's high-security prison on the Isle of Sheppey, Kent.

The chaplain said to me, 'Don't get your Bible out. Don't start preaching Scripture to these blokes, because they won't listen. We had a vicar in here last month who did that, and they all walked out.'

Having said that, he showed me into this room with a load of prisoners waiting. So, I had a split-second decision to make. I know we've said that we adapt our presentations to the scenario, but at the same time, we answer to God, not to men. I stood up in front of them, opened my Bible, and said, 'Right, lads, if it's all right with you, there's a lovely psalm I'd like to read.'

I read them Psalm 23 – 'The LORD is my shepherd' – and I read four more bits of Scripture after that, before telling my story and explaining the gospel.

Afterwards, a bloke came up to me and he leaned right in, grabbed me by the lapels, and pulled me close. I could literally smell what he'd had for breakfast. He said, right in my face, 'When you started speaking, I *hated* you . . . ' He paused, then carried on, 'I thought, "Here's another Bible basher . . . "' Then he leaned in even closer, still holding my collar, and said, 'But as you were speaking, I felt something change.'

By the end of the conversation, he was in tears and he was asking Jesus into his life.

That's the sort of thing that brings it home to me, that it's really not me doing this work. It's the Holy Spirit, and the power of the gospel. We just play our part. We go there and present Jesus Christ, crucified for our sins, and where there are hearts ready to hear, God works.

This bloke was in tears, and all I'd done was read five bits of Scripture and tell my story. I hadn't even lifted any weights. I'd gone in there pretty nervous, to be honest – I usually have

Ian with me. But the fact is, God uses our weakness. We've always gone in God's strength, not our own, and that's when God can work.

Ian

Some people respond immediately. They are at that point in their head where they are ready to say yes to Jesus. Others will listen to us, and be a bit more open to thinking about it afterwards, and it will be another step on a longer path. Prison chaplains have often said that a lot of blokes who never talked about spiritual things before will start having conversations with them after a visit from Tough Talk. Sometimes it's just about laying the very basics of a foundation.

I took Arthur to an STC once – a Secure Training Centre – for children who have committed crimes. They have both girls and boys in there, and they bring just five or ten in at a time, so you end up doing quite a lot of meetings. We do often use the weights for the younger people. So, I remember we'd done the weights with a group of boys and it had gone down well, then this group of girls came in – older teenagers – young women, really.

I was sitting there with Arthur and they were arguing on the way in, very unsettled, but the staff quietened them down. Arthur stood up, to start introducing himself. He said, 'I'm Arthur White . . .' and didn't get further than that, because the girls started shouting at each other, so he sat back down. The staff calmed them down, and when it was quiet again, Arthur stood up and continued, 'I'm from a group called Tough Talk . . .' and it all kicked off again – the girls started effing and blinding at each other, Arthur sat down again, and the staff shouted the girls down and tried to settle everyone down once more.

Arthur got up for a third time. 'We're a Christian charity, who . . .' and this time the girls started full-on fighting! They were grabbing each other's hair, they were kicking and pushing. The staff were trying to pull them apart. It was chaos. We just had to sit down again, and the prison officers decided to pull the plug.

I think that was the only meeting we've ever had where we didn't actually have the meeting.

Arthur

As the staff were taking them back out, though, the girls were gutted. They were saying, 'Oh no, sorry, we really want to stay!' They were really upset at themselves for ruining the opportunity. But they didn't have any self-control.

That's the only time I can remember that we didn't even get past our introductions.

Ian

Right from the start I had prisoners writing to me after we did prison visits. Sometimes they would ask questions, or tell me how our presentation had affected them. Sometimes they would tell us they responded and prayed the prayer, and they wanted to know what to do next.

It still happens now, when we visit prisons. Often I'll send them my book *Christ the Body Builder*,[1] which is all about spiritual disciplines to help you build a relationship with God. I'll always suggest they talk to the chaplain and get involved in prison fellowships.

What really excites me, though, is not just when someone responds, but when they start following Christ. There was one guy who wrote me a letter saying that he'd listened to our presentation, and then read the Tough Talk book I'd given him afterwards, which would have been our testimony book.[2] He said he prayed the prayer at the back of the book to give his life to Jesus. He told me that everything had changed, and he said, 'I've decided to become a soldier for Christ in prison.'

I've always remembered that phrase, because that really sums up what I do this for.

The guy really did start telling everyone in prison about Jesus, and became part of a fellowship group. When he came out, that group linked him up with a church, and the church discipled him. Last time I heard, he had become the leader of a church in the North of England somewhere.

Arthur

We're not soft on anyone. You feel for these guys and girls, but we don't say, 'Poor you, what a hard time you've had.' We always say that every single person has failed God and come up short compared to his standards. But for every single person, there is hope because Jesus died to forgive you, and release you from the things you've done wrong in the past. He can give you the hope of eternal life.

We sometimes say to people, 'There's a moment, and that moment is now.'

In a sense, if you don't make a decision for God, then you've made a decision against him.

But there's another sense in which there might be a lot of moments that build up towards an actual decision for Christ.

Sometimes a person has to go on their own journey, go through a process, until it's the right time for them to make a genuine decision and commitment to Jesus.

We like to keep the doors open. It's not one session that's got to do all the work. I call it breaking down the barriers to the godless.

David's story

My name's David York. I'm from Glasgow in Scotland.

I was heavily involved in a life of gang violence from the age of 15. I started carrying a knife at the age of 17 and if you carry a knife, after a while you start using it. We would get into endless fights. We would hit people over the head with bricks, or with bottles. More than once, I used my knife on someone. Whatever we could do, we did it. We had enemies and if we saw them, we would fight them.

If I got nicked, I'd sometimes start straight off on the police officer, headbutting him, breaking his nose, spitting, biting, whatever I could do. As soon as I was arrested for one thing, I did a load more things, so there were always numerous charges on the sheet by the time we got to the station.

I first saw Tough Talk in 2009 in Polmont YOI. It was early on in my faith journey. In fact, I wouldn't have known I was on a faith journey then. I didn't know that God was drawing me in.

I remember two or three really muscly guys talking about steroid abuse. I didn't reflect much on the faith element, I just remember thinking, 'Those were wild stories!' How these guys from the East End had been into violence and drugs, steroid abuse, gyms, powerlifting, had won all these titles, got themselves in complete messes and then had their lives turned right around – I thought that was wild.

It would be ten years later that I saw them again, and this time I'd be picking them up at the airport to take into a prison with me!

I didn't become a Christian when I saw Tough Talk, but it affected me. I became a Christian aged 21, around two years after. I had been in Polmont, then Barlinnie in Glasgow, then got transferred to HMP Kilmarnock. The chaplain at Kilmarnock was great. He invited me to their fellowship, and I got to know him and they helped me explore the faith.

Life slows down in prison. You have time to reflect. Outside, I'd be endlessly selling, dealing, running, fighting, using – it was manic. When I was inside, I'd sober up and get fit. I would think clearly. I didn't need to look over my shoulder.

People are more open in prison. They've hit rock bottom. They can't pretend. They are looking for change, but they don't know how. They know their life is going in a bad direction, but they don't know what to do about it.

In HMP Kilmarnock, I started reading the Bible, and I read books about people's lives being changed by God. I started going to chapel, and they often had people coming in with testimonies. It was one of those times that I answered a call and I gave my life to Christ.

After I left prison, though, I got sucked back in. I kept on with the drug use, the dealing, the alcohol and the violence – all the nonsense again. I genuinely had made a commitment, but I couldn't sustain it on the outside. In 2012 I got sent back to prison.

I recommitted my life to God, and when I got out this time, I decided to get serious. No more slipping back into the old ways. I reconnected with church. I got baptised. I signed up for a two-year Christian leadership course at Bible college, and suddenly I was surrounded by Christians.

I wanted to saturate myself with God and his people. I knew I could get sucked back in if I only had the old mates around, and the culture of violence, gangs and crime.

After Bible college, I joined a team that was planting a church in a deprived area of Glasgow. Then a friend and I set up a church plant in the area I grew up in.

I remember a police car drawing alongside me one day, the window winding down. 'Hello, David, we've heard you're a minister,' they said. 'We don't hear your name round much these days.'

What they meant was, 'We haven't heard your name around the station every day like we used to – you've stopped committing crime.'

I'm now the project manager of Prison Fellowship Scotland,[3] reporting to the director. I manage 170 volunteers who go into prisons. I recruit, support, liaise with prisons and chaplains, launch Alpha courses,[4] preach and run Bible study groups.

I had been running my own café, but I sold my business so that I could do this full-time. I've been to every prison in Scotland. I am sharing the gospel with people who are in the same situation I used to be in, and I love that. God's given me an opportunity to do something I'm passionate about, full-time, with a salary. I'm so blessed. And I now work with Tough Talk. A couple of times a year I speak to Arthur or Ian, and we work out dates for them to visit prisons up here.

I think one of the reasons they've been going so long is that they can tilt with changing policies and outlooks. They don't just come in to Bible bash. They also have genuinely interesting stories, and plenty to say about staying off steroids. They aren't threatening to a secular organisation like the Scottish

Prison Service – they're authentic, relevant and honest. They say and do things that prisoners relate to. They reach men that wouldn't otherwise get reached. They don't go all heavy on the altar call. They will say a prayer, then say, 'If you said that prayer with us, let us know.' So, it's not all about drawing attention, raising hands and counting how many people responded. I think that's good. It's a tactful way of doing things within the Scottish Prison Service.

I think it's important just to sow as many seeds as we can, and then leave things to God. The Holy Spirit is at work, convicting people of their sin. That's what happened to me. I got to a point where I was completely broken by my sin. I remember being at a conference, sitting with some other Christians. I was breaking down, tears rolling down my face, gutted at the wrong I had done. But this is the amazing thing – there was no condemnation. Not from the people I was with, and not from God. No judging. The Holy Spirit was showing me my sin, gently, and I was realising it. I wanted God to change my life for me. But what I really needed was forgiveness. And to find forgiveness, I had to go through repentance.

I'm so grateful to God now. I'm not a prisoner, and I say that in two ways. I'm not physically a prisoner, which is just amazing – I literally thought that's all I ever had to look forward to in life. But more importantly, I'm not a prisoner to my sin. I'm free.

When I was without clothes, you gave me something to wear. When I was sick, you cared for me. When I was in prison, you came to visit me.

Matt. 25:36, ERV

Chapter Three

A New Heart and a New Spirit

> I will give you a new heart and put a new spirit within you;
> I will take the heart of stone out of your flesh and give
> you a heart of flesh. I will put My Spirit within you and
> cause you to walk in My statutes . . .
>
> *Ezek. 36:26–27a, NKJV*

Ian

I didn't have a very normal upbringing, but there was love in it. I had four brothers and two sisters – seven of us all together, most from different fathers. We all lived with my mum. She was a bit eccentric. She was into pretty much anything and everything.

It was chaos in our house, it was havoc a lot of the time. It was dysfunctional. We were the family you didn't want to live next door to. In fact, my mum had put a sign up above our front door, that said 'Beware of the Kids'.

I remember one time, for some reason, some of us had decided to tie my baby brother to the bannisters and dangle him over the stairwell. I can't remember why we did that. We didn't have mobile phones to amuse us in those days . . . We'd sort of tied him to something from his clothes, and he was dangling upside down over the stairs, and we thought that was hilarious. Until he started screaming. So, my mum came to see what was going on, and of course she started screaming as well.

'Get 'im down! Get 'im down!' she yells, and starts hitting us with her hairbrush.

So, we're trying to untangle the baby from mid-air and get him back down again, but we can't manage, and he's swinging to and fro over the stairs. Then my older brother appears from somewhere, with a tea towel. He spins up the tea towel into a whip, and he starts whipping us – dancing round behind us, whipping our backsides while we're trying to get the baby down. And then, because my mum's come running in and started screaming, all the dogs come running in after her. My mum didn't just have one kid, she had seven kids. And she didn't just have one dog, she had about seven dogs as well. So they've all come in, and they're running round barking, biting each other. So you've got seven dogs, six kids, a tea towel, a yelling Mum with a hairbrush, and a screaming, dangling baby spinning round over the stairwell. And at that moment the doorbell rings.

My sister had mental health issues and she never used to answer the phone or open the door. But this particular day, because we're all busy fighting and yelling and trying to untangle the baby over the stairs, my sister goes to the door. She opens up the door, and there's a woman standing there.

I think what happened was, the woman was looking upwards, reading the 'Beware of the Kids' sign above the door, so when my sister opens the door, she just sees this tall woman with a neck and no face, and she freaks out and screams.

The woman looks down at the child screaming at her, then she looks in through the front door. There's a lady running round with a hairbrush, a load of boys wrestling and whipping each other, seven crazy dogs, and a baby dangling over the stairs. And the woman faints. She stone-cold faints – bang! – down over our doorstep.

Well, even the dogs stop barking at this point. But my mum yells, 'Quick! Drag her in! She might be a social worker!'

For a split second, we all think, 'This could be the moment we get taken into care.' However, it turned out, once she came round, that she was an Avon lady! I don't know how long she kept working for the Avon after that particular episode. She certainly never came to our door again.

If you think my childhood was chaotic, my adult life became even more so.

I grew up in a very similar part of London to Arthur. Right near Upton Park, which was West Ham's ground back then. I bunked off school, it held no interest for me. I was a bit of a bully. I was excluded from school once or twice. But I loved training.

I started to go to a gym in Forest Gate, east London, and began to lift the weights at about 13 years of age. I left school with no qualifications. I met some people who were into bodybuilding and I was captivated. I was intrigued by the techniques, the competitions, the sheer strength. I also loved the banter and the camaraderie of the guys training together.

I was competing as a body builder by about the age of 16. At 17 I was placed second in the Junior Mr England. At 18, I won the Essex Bodybuilding Championship.

I loved winning. Competing became everything to me. I was building serious muscle. At a height of 5ft 8in, I weighed

17 stone. I got into some competitions, got noticed, but I had yet to win anything major.

I was sitting in the gym one day and my friend said to me, 'Ian, if we want to take this further, we need to get on the anabolic steroids.'

So I started experimenting with steroids.

At the age of 19, I won the Junior South Coast of Britain competition, in Portsmouth. After that, I started using steroids a bit more seriously.

The first time I'd used them, I'd made incredible gains, so I thought if I carried on, then the increase in performance would continue as well, but it doesn't work that way. It starts having less effect, so you start thinking about taking more and more. I started injecting rather than just taking tablets. I thought I was in control. I wasn't.

Steroids are a synthetic hormone. They're a great drug if prescribed by a doctor. But if you're a young man and you start using anabolic steroids, and then abusing them, you're going to pay with the side effects of that. Steroids are basically testosterone. A young man will produce naturally 30mg or 40mg of testosterone a day. At the height of my addiction, I would be taking, synthetically, up to 500mg a day.

The following year, I was placed second in the Northern British Championships, then at the age of 21 I moved into the senior category. I won the South East British Championship, and came third in the British finals.

I didn't do so well in the following years, placing second and third, but I qualified for the World Championships around the age of 23. However, I was unable to go in the end. The health issues and injuries I was suffering from as a result of steroid use kept me from competing.

I seriously damaged my kidneys as a young man. I ended up having an operation because of the steroid use. I came out of hospital after that operation, and carried on taking them. I was urinating blood, I was suffering awful pain, but I was carrying on.

I have now been drug-free for more than thirty years. Yet, I still wake up with kidney pain because of the damage I did back in those days. I wanted to keep winning, and I was addicted.

I cheated in my sport, and I abused and misused steroids for eight years of my life. For four of those years I was using continually. Eight years of addiction. It messes with your body, it messes with your mind, and it costs a lot of money.

I was sitting in the gym one day; there was this scary individual that I often trained with. Bald head, chewed-up face, scars all over it, gold tooth. They used to call him Mad Dog. He pulled me aside and said, 'Ian, do you want to work with me on the door tonight, son?'

They used to call them bouncers in those days. Nowadays, you call them door supervisors. You have to pass an exam to be a door supervisor now. You learn a bit of Health and Safety, you pay a bit of tax, you get a licence and you're registered with the police. It's a serious business. It wasn't like that all those years ago. It was this scary gangster who saw that I was big and muscular offering me some work and frightening the life out of me. I didn't want to do it, but the trouble was, I needed the money. I needed it for the drugs.

He went on, 'Double bubble, son . . . Double the money if you come and work with me tonight.'

So I said, 'Yeah, maybe I'll have a bit of that.'

'Nice one. I'll pick you up later, son.'

He picked me up that night, and took me to this pub on Roman Road, east London. It was Christmas Eve. I remember sitting in the car with him before we went in. He was looking at me; I think he felt a bit sorry for me. I was expecting a bit of a safety briefing or something, but all he did was pull out a truncheon, and handed it to me, saying, 'Stick this in your jacket, boy. You're going to need this tonight.' Then he took me into the pub and said, 'Here, I'm going to introduce you to your colleagues . . . ' And he introduced me to this motley crew of men.

'This is Dave the Bus . . . '

'Alright Dave, how are you?' I sort of offered my hand, hoping I'd get it back in one piece.

'And this is One-Eyed Mark.'

'Alright Mark, nice to meet you.'

I worked with those characters for about eight years. They became my mates, and I became part of that world. We were in and out of trouble the whole time. There was a lot of violence. I'm not proud of that. During that period I turned my back on anyone who cared for me or loved me. I believe, over that time, I lost even the capacity to love or be loved. I got the appetite for hatred and violence. That was my life.

I began to have nightmares. Really oppressive, frightening nightmares. They were affecting my life. I never wanted to go to bed in case they came again. I would wake up sweating and shivering, my heart pounding like a piling machine.

Eventually, I told another guy on the door about it. Turned out he was a Christian. He invited me to church.

I went along – somewhat reluctantly – and to be honest, I thought it was a cult, to begin with. Even at the end of the service, I had no idea, really, what was going on. I'd never seen anything like it in my life. It was an Elim Pentecostal church[1] in Canning Town, east London. I vowed I'd never go back there. I just didn't like the place. I drew a line under it, carried on with life as before, and kept having the nightmares.

I continued my violent life, and the steroid use. However, slowly but surely, God was getting hold of me.

I had married my girlfriend, Valerie, and she was a Christian. I hadn't told her about the nightmares, preferring to keep them to myself, but one night, they were just too much. I woke up in the early hours sweating, my heart palpitating, totally freaked out by these evil dreams. I had to tell her. Valerie asked if she could pray, and I agreed. She did so, in Jesus' name, and almost instantly, the nightmares were replaced with a sense of peace.

I got involved in a massive fight one night with another group of doormen who we had a feud with. I got squirted with ammonia while getting beaten up. My pal who I was with – his name was Es – had a pickaxe handle smashed over his head. They nearly killed him. We were both rushed to hospital, and the medical staff performed emergency surgery on Es. They put metal plates in his head, and wired up his jaw.

It was the worst it had got. Seeing Es at the end of his tether, I surprised myself by suggesting we go to church together. Even more surprising, Es agreed. Early morning, I went round to his place, picked him up and took him to this church I'd been to before – in fact, it was a school building that this church was meeting in. It was the same stuff – music, speaking, prayer – and I felt just as uncomfortable as the first time. But at the end of the meeting, I found myself talking to a geezer called Tony. Tony told me how he'd become a Christian in prison – and it had transformed his life. His story made sense to me. He was someone I could relate to.

Then my friend Es got completely healed of his injuries, at a church meeting at Kensington Temple in Notting Hill Gate – a church that Tough Talk would end up working with many times. That meeting changed Es's life. The man speaking at the meeting prayed for Es's healing, and his whole head, jaw and eye were completely healed. Amazingly, God also enabled Es to forgive the people who had injured him, and he committed his life to Jesus. You couldn't be one of Es's friends and not know about this. I remember every time I saw him, he was smiling, and I'd never seen him smile before.

So it was a process with me and God – starting to understand, starting to believe – but there was one particular moment which I believe is when I surrendered my life to him.

I'd just been involved in another fight, and I was sitting alone in my car. I was about 25 years old at this point. A fight had broken out in the nightclub earlier that day. I'd chucked out the troublemakers, but they came back later on and petrol-bombed the place. Me and the lads I was working with didn't think much of that, so we tooled up, chased them down the road, and laid into them a bit.

It was the sort of thing that happened all the time, but on this occasion, something was different.

I was sitting in my car, covered in blood. I felt an incredible sense of guilt – which I hadn't felt before. I'd been thinking about God, and church, and my pal Es. I'd been thinking, 'If God can do that for such a dangerous, violent individual like Es . . . if God can heal him . . . can God sort me out too?'

I sat in my car and I said, 'Jesus, if you're real, would you sort me out? Would you forgive me for the scumbag that I am? Would you forgive me for what I've done?'

And at that moment I felt something cracking in my heart. I felt a warmth all over my body.

The Bible says, 'I will turn your heart of stone into a heart of flesh and pour my Spirit in you.'[2] I believe God's Spirit touched my life that night. Did I deserve it? No, I deserved hell. I was a horrible young man. Everything I did was wrong. But that night, I repented of my sin and made Jesus the Lord of my life. I drove home and I had a miracle. I fell asleep. I hadn't slept in weeks, and I remember waking up the next day with a new kind of peace. I immediately thought, 'Is that God? God, are you that real?'

I felt so different. Completely different. I was born again[3] – though I wouldn't have known that phrase myself.

I went back to the church I'd first gone to. I remember sitting down in the back row, and they started to worship. I thought, 'Oh no, I'm going to run again. I can't stand this music!' But in fact, as they started to worship, I felt different to before. I was looking at the Christians, thinking, 'Actually, these are quite nice people. Why was I thinking they were all brainwashed?'

They were singing a song called, 'You Laid Aside Your Majesty'.[4] It describes how Jesus willingly allowed himself to be put to death, then rose again, making forgiveness available to all those who believe in him. As I started to sing that, it began making some sense – that God himself came into the creation and died for my sins. I remember tears running down my face as I was connecting with Jesus Christ and the gospel.

At the end of the service, I bumped into Tony again. I was talking to him about what happened to me, because I didn't really understand it. He said, 'Ian, God is a Spirit. The Spirit of God has touched your life.' Then he said, 'You've got a choice now, mate. You can ignore God, and keep on as before.

Or you can repent – turn away from your sins and go the other way.'

I couldn't go back to the madness that was my life. I prayed with Tony. I repented of the crime, and the violence. I stopped going my own way, and decided to live life God's way. I'd had a taste of God's love and forgiveness, and it was all I wanted. I was free.[5]

I will also put a new spirit in you to change your way of thinking. I will take out the heart of stone from your body and give you a tender, human heart. I will put my Spirit inside you and change you so that you will obey my laws.

Ezek. 36:26–27a, ERV

Chapter Four

The Cold English Sea

All have sinned and fall short of the glory of God . . .

Rom. 3:23, NKJV

Ian

We got invited down to Bournemouth one summer, in the late 1990s. It was a beautiful afternoon, and I remember hanging around on Bournemouth seafront, eating fish and chips, waiting for it to be time for the event we were speaking at. The sun was out and there were crowds of people around – eating ice creams, playing ball games, running in and out of the sea.

When we got to the meeting that evening, it was in a little scout hut, and there were about thirty people there. I remember thinking, 'What are we doing here? There are so many people on the beach . . . '

That's where my appetite for street evangelism started.

Arthur

The evangelist Dominic Muir[1] describes street evangelism as being like going into the cold English sea for a swim. You want to do it, because you know you love the ocean. But you still have to force yourself to go in. At first, when your body enters the cold water, it's grim, it's a shock. But then the further in you go, the better it becomes. You keep going, and suddenly you're swimming, and it's the most glorious, refreshing thing you could ever think of.

Our love for Jesus compels us to go and tell people about him. And it's a great privilege to do so. But we still have to summon up the courage to get up there and get started sometimes! Yet once we have started, and we're hitting the flow, it's the best thing in the world.

Ian

A church in Bath invited us to do outreach on the streets with them, around the year 2000. It's a great city for street preaching – lots of lovely outdoor spaces.

Joe, Arthur and myself were all there, and two or three other Tough Talk guys. We'd got ourselves a small, portable PA kit by then, so we set it up in a square. I turned on a bit of music. It wasn't Christian music, just something with a bit of a beat – in fact, I think it was a remix of an Elvis song.

We started setting up. We were going to and from the van with our bars and weights, and a crowd started forming. People began to get interested. Kids were asking me, 'What's going on here?'

We'd done a few bits and pieces of street work by then, and I'd been thinking for a while about street entertainers, and how they do a lot of preamble rather than going in cold. So, when these youngsters asked the question, I started giving out some teasers, whetting their appetite. I was saying things like, 'Hang about, kids. You'll see some strongman stuff in a bit.'

By the time we were set up, there were sixty people standing there, watching and waiting!

We'd been doing street outreach for four years or so by then – but Bath was the first time I remember putting it all together. There were five or six of us at the front, and once we'd done the introductions, as we started powerlifting, there must have been about two hundred people watching.

I thought to myself, 'These people are involved with us already – so why not get them fully involved?' I said to the crowd, 'Right, who wants to come and have a go?'

We had the bench press set up, and you could see a few of the guys in the crowd were interested, so we did a bit of encouragement, a bit of banter: 'Is that your dad? Do you think he could lift this thing a few times? You want him to have a go?'

We made it into a little competition. We had a laugh – a bit of chat with the fellas lifting, a bit of light-hearted commentary on their attempts at the bench. Suddenly we had that extra layer of interest. It's not just watching some random strong guys lift weights, it's also seeing your own dad, your own husband or friend going against some other dads or husbands or friends, seeing who can bench press the most. There's a new dynamic.

We were having a lot of fun and of course, the crowd thought it was just some entertainment. Then we started the testimonies. And they kept listening. Then we started preaching the gospel. And they kept listening. They pretty much all stayed, right to the end.

It wasn't that we'd kidnapped their dads to have a go at the lifting! What had happened was, we had built rapport. We'd established a bit of relationship with those people. They'd seen us setting up, we'd talked to them and answered their questions. They'd seen us lift and they'd seen each other lift. We were chatting, commenting and joking with people. They had got to know us a little bit, and they could see we weren't nutters. And from there, it was like we had a springboard into the really important stuff.

I remember Arthur standing there telling his story: 'I'm a four-time world champion powerlifter, but everything I had, I lost in four years of madness.' And they were hanging on his every word.

We realised after that, that we had a bit of a formula. You get people's interest, and hook them in – which is what the weights do. Then you flip it, and give testimonies – telling the stories of what God did in your own life, and they're interested. Then you flip it again, and you say, 'Do you know what, this stuff isn't just about us. It's about you too. It's relevant – because Jesus is real, and he wants to bring forgiveness and peace to you as well.' And there you go, you've preached the gospel on the streets.

It was always about Jesus, and always about reaching the lost. I don't care about looking the most professional, or winning points, or how well anyone can lift. I care about what works best in getting people's attention and connecting them with Jesus.

I've done outreach where I've talked about healing and miracles, and offered to pray for people on the streets, but it doesn't draw a crowd in Britain. People just think you're crazy and hurry past, or head in the opposite direction.

I still go out on a soap box occasionally and have my say, but the fact is, we hit on a format which worked. We went out with the weights, chatted to the crowd, told our stories, then preached the gospel and people listened. We started making appeals on the streets and people responded. People were meeting God on the streets, standing there and saying, 'Yes, I want to change, I want Jesus in my life,' putting their hands up in public, letting us pray for them.

So, we've been pretty much doing that for the last thirty years. Why would you mess with it, when you can see it works?

Arthur

People have said to us, 'Where did you get your training on public speaking?' But we've never had any training. I had a guy come up to me once after an event and say, 'The way you structure your presentation, it's straight out of a textbook, it's brilliant!'

I just said, 'Thanks, mate, that's lovely.'

It doesn't bother me – I just do what I can see is getting people's attention. Ian's an avid reader, and he's obsessed with the old-fashioned evangelists. He loves that stuff! But apart from that, we haven't read any textbooks; we've just observed what works with people and learned as we go along.

We have been doing this a long, long time. We're still motivated to do it to the best of our ability. Whatever God uses to reach people with his love, that's what we'll keep doing.

Ian

I think open-air stuff is probably the most exciting aspect of what we do – the most exhilarating, and the most nerve-wracking!

We did the Notting Hill Carnival quite a few years in a row. We worked with Kensington Temple, which is a large Elim church in west London.

I remember one time in particular, it was evening. We'd been out on the street all day. We were back at the church, we'd packed the weights away, it was late. The music was still going on, on the stage that Kensington Temple had put up, and the evangelism pastor came into the church.

'The police have told us to stop the music,' he said.

'Fair enough,' I thought. 'It's late, we're pretty much done.'

But the pastor turned to me and said, 'Ian, you need to go out there. Get the music turned off, and preach the gospel.'

There were about three thousand people out there. Literally. The streets were packed. By this stage, many of them were off their heads from drinking and taking recreational drugs all day. I was knackered already from the four or five presentations we'd already done.

There were stories circulating about fights, stabbings, assaults – all the carnage and fallout from a festival when the families have gone home – and the last place I really wanted to be was back out there again. But from the look on the pastor's face, I didn't have much choice.

I went up onto the platform, and there was this writhing mass of people in front of me, dancing to the gospel reggae music that was playing out of the church's speakers. The air was filled with the pungent stench of cannabis. There were mounted police in various places flanking the crowd, and you could see they were getting a bit agitated. Their horses were shifting nervously.

I picked up the microphone, and I remember saying to the DJ, 'Can you stop the music, mate?' Then I said to the crowd,

'Look, guys, we're a church. This is Kensington Temple, who have put up this stage and provided this music for you.' I looked out at this rolling sea of drunken, stoned people and took a breath. 'I'm gonna tell you my story.'

I started sharing my story. How I'd been a doorman in the East End, in tough parts of London, how I'd been involved in a world of violence, crime and fear. Then I thought, 'In for a penny, in for a pound,' and I gave them the gospel.

I told them that I'd found forgiveness from God. I told them that when I'd met Jesus, I'd cried out for mercy, turned away from all the wrong I'd been involved in, and found a completely different way to live. I told them I believed that Jesus Christ was God's Son, and that one day all of us would have to give an account of our lives to the ultimate Judge. I gave them the whole lot – heaven, hell, judgement.

When I stopped, I realised that they were all staring at me. A silence had come over this massive crowd, and they were all looking at me intently. The place was packed, no one was moving. I wasn't sure what to do, so I carried on.

'You can repent, and ask Jesus into your life. If you want to do that, then pray this prayer with me.' And I prayed the prayer. Then I said, 'We've got Bibles here. If you prayed that prayer and you want a Bible, then come forward.'

Suddenly, people were coming forward. Loads of them. They wanted Bibles, they wanted to ask questions, they wanted to tell us they'd prayed the prayer.

One girl simply said to me, 'What just happened?' She was open-mouthed and wide-eyed. She said, 'I just felt enormous peace and love when you prayed that prayer. What happened? What is that?'

I said, 'That's the Holy Spirit. The presence of God.'

She was spot on. There was a tangible sense of the Holy Spirit. I still find it incredible, to be honest. There was this godless place – people just hedonistically pleasing themselves; this darkness – both literal and spiritual – and it felt like the last place that a message would break through to anyone. Yet God's power came.

I was not at all confident when I stepped up onto that platform. I'd basically been given the job of stopping the party, with a crowd of thousands who'd been partying all day. I didn't know how to go about it, or how people would react. I was pretty nervous as I told the DJ to cut the music, and started talking into that massive, empty, threatening silence. But God moved.

Kensington Temple is a praying church. I know they were backing me up that night. I just went and did my thing – did as I was told, if you like. I told my story, I said my piece, and God in his grace came and met people, and loved people and saved people.

You can never predict how it's going to go out on the streets. Much more recently, I was out in Waltham Abbey with Joe, preaching. The pastor who booked us had seen us at an event years before, and he had become a Christian that very night, watching us preach. But on this particularly occasion, there didn't seem much interest on the streets at all. We lifted, we gave our testimonies, and there wasn't much reaction. It all felt a bit flat, to be honest, and Joe and I wondered whether it had been worth it.

However, when it came to Sunday, there was a service at the church, and a load of new people turned up – they were people who'd seen us out on the streets on Saturday. They'd been given a flier about the church, by the church members who had come out with us, and they came along.

You might have a real laugh one day, and a big crowd, but everyone goes home and forgets about it. Or you might have a really quiet day, when it feels like no one's responding, but actually, when they arrive home, they get down on their knees and start talking to God. You just can't tell.

Street evangelism can feel like the least fruitful work, because in Britain it very much goes against the culture. It's not normal to stand up in a random public place and start telling people about your life and your beliefs. I believe there's a spirit of intimidation out there that stops British Christians speaking out about their faith. There's something in our spiritual atmosphere over here. It's a bit like in the Bible, when Peter says to Jesus, 'I'll fight and go to death with you, Lord,'[2] but then a few hours later, he's denying Jesus to a little maidservant – he's suddenly too embarrassed to say he's a follower. That atmosphere can hinder Christians in Britain.

We've done street evangelism in a number of other countries, and it's really different to here. Whether it's Romania, or South Africa, or even Harlem or the Bronx, if you turn up on the streets with some music and some weights, there will be a crowd. You won't have to work for it in the same way. People aren't embarrassed to be curious.

Arthur

Even though I've been doing this for thirty years, I still get nervous and apprehensive. It was the same when I was doing the powerlifting, mind you. I remember my wife saying to Emma and James, 'Keep out of the way for a bit, kids, your dad's got a competition coming up.' But once I was up there on the platform lifting, I was in my element.

It's similar with going on the streets – once you're there and trusting in the Holy Spirit it's a wonderful thing, a fantastic feeling. But you sometimes have to battle through a bit to get there.

Street evangelism is the riskiest kind of work in some ways – the highest stakes, perhaps, especially in Britain. We've had stuff thrown at us – oranges, bottles, that sort of thing. We've had plenty of people shout and swear – though that's a newer development. When we first started, it was mostly polite refusal to take any notice, but the culture has changed.

We've been on beaches, we've been on the backs of trailers, we've been on ski slopes. We've been dropped off by pastors in completely dead-end parts of unknown towns and left to get on with it. We've preached to men, women, children, vegetables, brick walls and seagulls. Literally. If no one comes, we'll preach to the seagulls.

We have worked with lots of people who don't want to hear – who shout, or leave, or take offence. But so what? We're not there for the people who want to turn their backs and reject us. We're certainly not up for forcing anyone to listen to us. We're there for the ones who might just have half an ear out – the ones where God is working, even though they might not know it yet.

At the end of the day, in a funny way, we're not really there for people at all. First and foremost, we're there for Jesus.

Chris's story (Part one)

Back in 2006, I was involved in Notting Hill Carnival, and that was crucial in my faith journey.

As a young lad, I didn't like myself a lot. I disliked my body. I hated what I saw in the mirror. I had ginger hair, too – one of just two ginger boys in the school – and back then, that was not much fun. I got laughed at and stuff.

In my bedroom, I had dumbbells and some bodybuilding magazines, and I'd look through them and think, 'I wanna look like that. Who's going to mess with those guys?' So, I started training in my bedroom, trying to change myself. Trying to make myself feel better.

When I left school I became a mechanic, and then my car obsession was what really took over.

I was married when I was young, for about seven years, and we have two girls together. We had an OK marriage. I was working a lot just to provide and make ends meet.

I felt a lot of pressure to look good. My wife was into Jean-Claude Van Damme,[3] which didn't help. I pursued kick-boxing for a couple of years, trained hard, won a few competitions. Then I had a car accident. They said I'd damaged my neck, and shouldn't be taking kicks to the head any more. So, I had to give up the kick-boxing. I felt like my life was over.

I started training at a gym in Watford. It was under a car park and it stank to high heaven. It was a hole. But it was one of those metal-weights, blood-sweat-and-tears sort of *Rocky* gyms that really appealed to me.

I met this guy. He was bench-pressing. And when I saw the weight he was bench-pressing, I couldn't believe it. I went over to talk to him, and we had a bit of a chat. I asked him, 'Am I going to get bigger?'

He said, 'Well, you've got to eat the protein, and if you want to take something extra, that's up to you.'

So, I asked him to get me something, and he set me up with my first course of steroids. I noticed it immediately, I really started putting more muscle on. So I was straight back to this guy, saying, 'When's my next course?' And of course that's how it goes. You keep wanting it. And once you realise you're not in control of it any more, it's too late. I tried different types – fast-acting, slow-acting. I was taking various tablets, every six hours, then I started injecting.

Long story short, my marriage broke down. I moved back to my parents, in Borehamwood. I was pretty broken, but after a couple of years, I met someone new, and things started looking up again.

The lady I met had been a Christian for some years, but she wasn't really following her faith. She'd had some issues, and had stopped going to church. But when we had been together a little while, she started thinking about her faith again. She wanted our relationship to be on a proper footing, she wanted to make things right.

We went to a coffee shop where we'd heard there was a church gathering, but it was closed. However, someone gave her a leaflet about Tough Talk at the Notting Hill Carnival. We went there, and they were doing their first presentation of the morning. We stayed, and watched. When they finished, we still stayed there, and we watched them do it again – two or three times during the day. My girlfriend pushed me to go and join in, and eventually I did.

They did the hammers first – two wooden hammers, about 2ft long. You have to stand with your arms outstretched sideways, a hammer in each hand, for as long as you can. It's very demanding. But I won the hammers, and then later, I did a log lift, and I won that as well. Ian presented me with my prize – a Tough Talk DVD. It had Arthur on it, Ian and two other men who were with Tough Talk at the time – telling their testimonies of their lives before and after God. I watched the DVD and I thought it was great. The stories were amazing and I could relate to a lot of the stuff. I watched it right through, then put it away.

Later that afternoon I was sitting in the garden. My brain was sort of ticking over, and I was drawn to watching the DVD again. I couldn't work out why. So, I watched it again, and of course there's a prayer at the end of it. The message was along the lines of, 'If God can forgive people like us, then he can forgive you too', and the prayer guided you in asking for God's forgiveness. So, I said that prayer.

When you say that prayer, some people have a load of cartwheels and fireworks going on. I didn't. But I definitely did feel different. I felt a sense of peace. I wasn't totally sure what had happened. I told my girlfriend what I'd done, and she said, 'Oh, you've just become a Christian!'

All have sinned and are not good enough to share God's divine greatness.

Rom. 3:23, ERV

Chapter Five

On the Battlefield

Put on the whole armor of God, that you may be able to
stand against the wiles of the devil.

Eph. 6:11, NKJV

Ian

I first started reading the Scriptures to keep me alive.

I had come to faith, but I was still working as a doorman –
that was my living. It was a dangerous occupation. You never
knew where the next trouble was going to come from. So,
we were always tooled up – a knife here, a baseball bat there,
a couple of knuckledusters in your pocket. I'd been carrying
weapons, every day, for eight years.

When I came to faith, I was convicted to stop. I knew that's
what God wanted. I started getting rid of some of my weapons. But I felt vulnerable without them. I was still working in
the same place, with the same crazy people.

I started reading Psalm 91:

> He that dwelleth in the secret place of the most High shall
> abide under the shadow of the Almighty. I will say of the Lord,
> He is my refuge and my fortress: my God; in him will I trust.
>
> *vv. 1–2, KJV*

I memorised practically the whole psalm, and I used to say
it to myself on the way to work, speaking the verses out loud
in the car.

> For he shall give his angels charge over thee, to keep thee in
> all thy ways. They shall bear thee up in their hands, lest thou
> dash thy foot against a stone.
>
> *vv. 11–12, KJV*

Those words were life to me. Instead of trusting in my
physical weapons to defend myself, I wanted to trust in my
heavenly Father to keep me safe. It wasn't easy. It was a battle.

Arthur

You might have noticed that Ian and I believe in heaven and hell.

We believe that there is good in the world, and there is
evil. Sometimes that evil is very obvious, but sometimes it's
invisible.

The Bible says, 'We wrestle not against flesh and blood, but
against principalities, against powers, against the rulers of the
darkness of this world, against spiritual wickedness in high
places' (Eph. 6:12, KJV). We're not here to fight against any human being, be it man, woman, child, politician, churchgoer,

gangster, thief, whatever. We're here to 'fight the good fight of faith' (1 Tim. 6:12, NKJV). When we go out to tell our testimonies, and share the good news of Jesus, we are standing against the evil influences that keep people bound up in fear, hatred, bitterness, addiction and violence.

We're here to serve a powerful God, who can bring freedom, truth and light to any life. So the weapons we fight with are not human weapons.

Ian

When I first worked on the door with Mad Dog, I bought a set of knuckledusters. They were unusual, in that they were made in a mould with a flat head. So, they sat flat across your knuckles, rather than with lumps and spikes and what-have-you. Brass knuckledusters. It was at a place called the Ilford Palais. My mate bought some, and I bought some.

I liked my knuckledusters. They were heavy, and they didn't leave holes in people's faces. So, I could pull one out, hit someone, put it back in my pocket, and nobody would even know I'd used it, because there wouldn't be any blood spurting out. It would just look like I'd had a good old punch. And I could throw that good old punch without breaking my hand – which was a significant bonus.

Fast-forward eight years, and I'd managed to get rid of all my weapons except one. I'd held on to this one knuckleduster. I knew it wasn't right, but there was a massive struggle going on inside me. I had made Jesus Lord of my life, and a lot of things had changed. I wanted to trust in God completely, I was praying that I would trust God completely, but I couldn't shift that thought: 'What if it kicks off tonight? Will I be safe?'

I'd started keeping my knuckleduster on the shelf above the bar, rather than in my pocket. I was really trying to be rid of it. I would hide it up there, so I wasn't carrying it, at least, but so that if a situation started, I could still reach up and grab it. I was so conflicted.

Then I got a call from Mad Dog.

"Ello, Ian, son. Listen, you ain't got those knuckledusters still, what we bought ten years ago, 'ave you?'

I said, 'Yeah, I have actually got one, Mad Dog. Why?'

'Well, it's like this, Ian. I got nicked the other night, and I had one of them on me . . . So I told the Old Bill that it was not a weapon, but gym equipment. You know how those knuckledusters have some holes, along the flat bit? Well, I told 'em it was the handle of a home-made chest-expander! I made out like I had springs to put through the holes, and another handle back home, and that I used it for training.'

'Right?' I said, wondering where this was all going.

'Thing is, Ian, they called my bluff. They told me, if I could produce the rest of the kit – the other handle, and the springs – then they would believe me, and let me have my knuckleduster back. Trouble is, I've only actually got one.'

He paused. 'You still got one, Ian?'

'You know what, Mad Dog,' I said, 'you're an answer to prayer! I've been praying that I'd get rid of this knuckleduster, now the Lord's sent you along to make it happen!'

Mad Dog wasn't sure about the prayer bit, but he was happy to take my knuckleduster off me. We arranged to meet up, and I handed it over. My last weapon. The last thing I'd been hanging on to from my old ways.

I watched Mad Dog drive off back to the police station to get back his 'home-made chest-expander,' and I actually laughed.

Within weeks of surrendering my last physical weapon, God took me away from that violent crew of door workers. Without any apparent reason, I got moved to a little place in Soho, working on the door of a club in Wardour Street. It couldn't have been more different. Instead of fighting and getting shot at, I was standing with businesspeople, going, 'Yeah, Greek Street's down that way, mate. Shall I call you a taxi?' I didn't see a fight in two years of working there.

I believe the Lord was waiting for me to trust him wholeheartedly. And when I was struggling, that final little nudge was sending Mad Dog, so I could give my knuckleduster up to him. Only then did God get me right out of that violent place, and settle me somewhere different. Never had Psalm 91 seemed more real: 'He will call upon me, and I will answer him: I will be with him in trouble; I will deliver him, and honour him' (Ps. 91:15, KJV).

Arthur

It's about what we hold on to, that separates us from God. If you're trusting in something else – even just a little bit – you are not free to fully follow God, and he can't use you fully.

Ian eventually came out of the world of door work, and I came out of the debt-collecting world, because we both knew that what we were doing was not the right way. So, at the right time, we packed it up and walked away. And then you are trusting in God, because apart from anything else, you've no longer got the income you were relying on.

But trusting in God alone is actually the very safest way to live.

We laid our earthly weapons down, and we learned to pick up heavenly weapons to enter into the spiritual battle, which is between good and evil – between life and death.

The top heavenly weapons on our list are prayer and reading the Bible. We won't apologise for going on and on about reading the Bible. The Bible is life. It is the Word of God. One of the psalms says, 'Your word is a lamp to my feet and a light to my path (Ps. 119:105, NKJV) and 'The law of thy mouth is better unto me than thousands of gold and silver' (v. 72, KJV).

Ian

I started with Psalm 91 when I was frightened for my life in that violent gang working on the doors. But from that, I realised that the Bible nourished my soul and equipped me for the battle. Thirty years on, I still read it every day.

I read the Bible because I want my life to be meaningful, because I want my marriage to be meaningful and enriched, because I want my work to make sense, and because it gives me life and understanding, truth and power. I want to be in the best condition to serve my Father.

You need to be aware of the spiritual battle. You don't need to be afraid of it, but you do need to be aware.

Back in 1995–96, in my very early years of ministry, before I met Arf, one of the main characters I worked with started having an issue with me. He could see some of the spiritual opposition we were facing, and he got nervous. He was talking to guys who worked with me, saying they were going to face attacks from the devil if they went out with me. This started making others scared and intimidated, and it was turning them against the work of Tough Talk. It got to the point where men were falling out with each other, dividing into camps.

It was like secondary school – 'if you go with Ian to a meeting, then you're not my friend any more' – that sort of thing.

I couldn't be doing with manipulative games. All I wanted was to preach the gospel. I said to the guys, 'Look, I'm not going to drag someone out and force them to preach with me, am I? Either come with me and help me preach the gospel, or don't. It's up to you. I'm going anyway.'

I would regularly take a team of six guys out to each event back then, and at one point, I had this particular meeting booked. But one by one, the lads started dropping out, and when it came to it, the meeting was just me and one other guy. I sort of shrugged, and off we went. It was a great meeting, really powerful – God was there, and people responded, even though it wasn't the big team I'd been planning.

Then the guy who had come – the only one who had come – rang me up the next day.

'Ian, I can't do this any more,' he said.

It turned out that on the way home that night, he ran into the bloke who had been criticising me, who asked him, 'Why are you still involved in this stuff? I thought you were my pal.' He was laying on the emotional pressure, and my mate couldn't hack it.

'I'm sorry, Ian,' he said to me on the phone. 'I've had enough. I'm pulling out.'

I was gutted. I felt so alone. I felt like Tough Talk had fallen apart as soon as it had started. I was really, really disappointed. The Bible says, in 2 Timothy 1:7: 'God has not given us a spirit of fear, but of power and of love and of a sound mind' (NKJV). I still don't really understand what went on back then. Those men were passionate about God, and still are now. And yes, there was sometimes spiritual opposition when we went out as Tough Talk, and that can be intimidating. But I think they let their fear take a hold of them, and the enemy took the opportunity to wield some emotional and spiritual manipulation.

I was left on my own, and I literally thought it was all over. But I remember very, very clearly, as I was driving home a few days later, having an amazing revelation.

I'm not a super-spiritual person. I don't get many visions or words of knowledge.[1] Sometimes, the Lord will put a particular verse on my heart, and that's about it. But that day, I was driving home, and I saw a big tree which had been cut right back. It had had most of its branches lopped off, quite severely, till it was just an ugly lump of a tree trunk. As I went past, though, I saw that it had lots and lots of tiny shoots growing out of it.

I remember saying to God, 'Wow, you really are amazing, Lord, that you can cut something right back like that, and yet there's loads of life springing out.' As soon as I had that thought, I just knew that it was the Lord talking to me about Tough Talk.

Within a few weeks, there was a guy called Steve who joined us. Then there was another bloke, Dave, and then Adam. And it was only a few months after that, that I got invited to the FGB event in London, and met Arthur.

So, I went from feeling totally alone, in a failed ministry, to having a group of guys who were totally up for it, bought into the vision, and sharing the passion. We didn't know it then, but that team would last for years and years. But we had to go through that pruning phase first.

Arthur

I think God's done that pruning with all of us individually, as well as with Tough Talk as a whole. There's lots of ways Ian, Joe and I have been 'pruned' by God over the years. It can be painful, but we shouldn't be surprised. It's in the Bible: 'He cuts off every branch in me that bears no fruit, while every branch that does bear fruit he prunes so that it will be even more fruitful' (John 15:2, NIV).

Me personally, I've had ongoing issues with my health. I am living with quite a bit of pain. I'm waiting for the possibility of four operations – two on my heart and two on my spine. I'm waiting for a scan on my brain that might lead to another operation.

I've relied on my physical strength in my life, and now that's being taken away from me. It comes as a shock that I have these physical limitations, and physical pain that stops me doing what I want to do. But I don't actually pray for God to take it away. I have spoken to God about it, and he has used my physical weakness to say, 'Arthur, you've got to be leaning on me, all the time, completely.'

Ian

To pretend that Christianity is a path to a rosy life is a nonsense, and dishonest. But that's not a reason to fear. Don't be afraid. Every time I go out on a mission, it's not a coincidence if my car breaks down, there's an unexpected bill, or something comes up with one of the kids that needs dealing with. That's happened many times to me, and many times to others who were ministering with Tough Talk.

You maybe don't go out for a bit, and things calm down again. Then you go out on another mission, and everything kicks off again.

Whether you're being attacked by evil, or the Lord's allowing things to happen in order to teach or strengthen you, or whether life is just getting at you, it doesn't really matter. The Bible says, 'I am strong in my weakness' (2 Cor. 12:10). So, it's not about somehow being victorious over these things, it's just about getting on and keeping going, and through your human weakness, God's divine strength can work.

In fact, in a funny way, the spiritual battle isn't some active way of taking the fight to the devil, it's much more about letting God work through you and strengthen you. It's about stepping out in his strength, laying down your own strength and everything else.

Us men often want to fix or sort something. We like to take action. But the main action for a soldier of Christ is to press in to him. Our fighting is getting closer to God, resting in God, trusting in God. As it says in Deuteronomy: 'The LORD himself goes before you and will be with you; he will never leave you nor forsake you' (Deut. 31:8, NIV); and in 2 Chronicles, God says to the king, Jehosaphat: 'Do not be afraid or discouraged because of this vast army. For the battle is not yours, but God's' (NIV).

Arthur

Everywhere we go, it feels like there will have been some sort of battle to get there. The door will open at the last minute. The prison governor will suddenly say, 'Yeah, that's OK, let them in.' Someone in authority will show us a moment of favour. The traffic will suddenly start moving. We've been running in the back of a tent just as someone's walking up onto the platform to introduce us, when an hour before we thought we were never gonna get there. We often seem to make it by the skin of our teeth. It's like *Mission Impossible*! It's not like we go jumping off the top of buildings and headbutting buses to prove that God is protecting us. But we are spurred on by our faith, and by the things we've seen God do. We always come back from events going, 'Praise the Lord, everything fell into place! That door! How did that open up? How did we get in there? How did we end up speaking to that group of people?'

We're constantly amazed at what God does through us. We just try and keep focused on the cross and focused on Jesus. The moment we stop trusting him, or start relying on ourselves, our own gifts, our own stories, that's going to be the end of Tough Talk. But, if we keep standing on the truth of God's promises – 'Don't worry, I'll give you the words to say; I'll be with you; I'll protect you; I'm by your side' – then God will keep doing his amazing business of salvation through our small, human efforts.

Ian

I was visiting a drug recovery programme a few years ago, and there were about eighty people there. I was sitting, praying before I was about to go out and speak, and these words popped into my head: 'God is able to save to the uttermost those that come to him by Jesus Christ.' I thought, 'Wow! Is that Scripture? Where's that come from all of a sudden? I think it sounds like Scripture.' I googled it, and it came up as Hebrews 7:25.[2] I thought to myself, 'I wonder why God has put that in my head.' And even as I was thinking that, a guy came over to me, and said, 'Ian! Do you mind if I talk to you quickly?'

'Yeah, go on, mate.'

'I'm not here for the meeting,' he said. 'I've actually been trying to find you guys, and I heard you were speaking here tonight. Years ago, you and Joe and Arthur spoke at a youth meeting that I was at. It was me and my best friend, Mark. He was 16 at the time. That night, both myself and my friend asked Jesus into our lives. Arthur gave us a Bible each.' He went on: 'The very next day, my best friend, Mark, went out on his motorbike, had an accident and died. I've always felt very strongly that the Lord used you guys to bring him to God, just in time, to save him to the uttermost.'

When someone tells you a story like that, it's very humbling. Because what did we do? We were simply obedient. We spoke God's words. Arthur prayed and gave a Bible, just like we do to anyone who comes forward for prayer. God did the saving. Only he knew what was going on.

I always take that verse wherever I go now – that God is 'able to save to the very uttermost'. It was beautiful, too, that this young man had wanted to come and tell us that story. He had tracked us down to share that with us – his certainty that his friend, who met such an early death, was nevertheless with Jesus.

There are spiritual forces that don't want us to do what we're doing. They don't want the name of Jesus to be preached, and they don't want people to be saved from perishing. But God's power is greater.

There are consequences of death without Christ. The Bible says, 'He who turns a sinner from the error of his way will save a soul from death' (Jas 5:20, NKJV).

We work sometimes with a church in Norwich called St Stephen's. It has a graveyard next to it, and when I walk down the path between the gravestones, it reminds me that we are in a very serious, eternal spiritual battle. The Bible says there's a time coming when all those in their graves will 'hear His voice and come forth – those who have done good, to resurrection of life, and those who have done evil, to the resurrection of condemnation' (John 5:28–29, NKJV). Yet the Scriptures also say that there are none who have done good – 'no, not one' (Rom. 3:10, NKJV). Only one is good and that's God himself, and Jesus is the Son of God who paid the price for our sins. He's the one that achieved goodness for us that we could not obtain for ourselves.

God has already won the battle, because Jesus conquered the grave – he rose from the dead. That may sound crazy, but he is the only person in history who, having died, lived again. He is 'the resurrection and the life' (John 11:25, NKJV). He defeated death itself, and those who put their trust in him will be with him in paradise.

You can't see what's happening in the spiritual realm. When someone turns up to a meeting, or lingers on a street listening, or sits in the prison chapel, you can't see what is going on in their hearts. Maybe it's a chance for their life to change. Maybe it's the last chance, and you're God's instrument at that moment. Who knows?

This is a matter of life and death for people, and if there's a chance God is going to use me, I'm going to make sure I'm in good condition for the battle.

Wear the full armor of God. Wear God's armor so that you can fight against the devil's clever tricks.

Eph. 6:11, ERV

Chapter Six

In the Ranks

> Now then, we are ambassadors for Christ, as though God
> were pleading through us: we implore you on Christ's
> behalf, be reconciled to God.
>
> *2 Cor. 5:20, NKJV*

Arthur

Ian, Joe and I are fighting spiritual battles, but we've also spent
a lot of time over the last thirty years with soldiers, sailors and
airmen in the physical Armed Forces, and we count that a
major privilege.

When a chaplain or a padre invites us in, we say yes, and
we take it as another opportunity. We go as God's ambassadors, on his behalf, to take his message. We do something
with the army or navy most years now, and have done since
the early 2000s. Like anything else, it started when somebody
enquired, and we said yes, and next thing we know, we're
standing in front of a whole battalion of uniformed soldiers,
telling them about Jesus!

Whatever your ethical view of armed conflict, for us it's
all about reaching people with the gospel. There's eternal life

available. That young lad in front of me could lose his life next week, and the Bible says those who 'call upon the name of the Lord shall be saved' (Rom. 10:13, KJV). That is an opportunity that we are not going to pass up.

Ian

Back in the 2000s, we did quite a bit of work on the military bases in Germany. If you were stationed in the British Army in Germany at the time, you could have your wives and kids living with you. The camps were amazing – like a miniature Britain out in Germany. You had the married quarters, the smaller houses for squaddies, your little Tesco for the groceries – all the things you needed.

We always started with a session in their gym. That was pretty similar to what we do in prisons, but weirdly, in the army, the guys interact less. They're drilled, and they've got their sergeant or whoever with them, so they're not quite at ease. You try and get a laugh out of them and it's hard work – it's not in their mindset. It's hard to know what they're thinking.

They probably have to be that way. Maybe they're trained not to give anything away. Or they're just drilled to do what they're told and no more. Or they think you're part of the establishment – they don't want to step out of line or look foolish. Whatever it is, it takes them a bit of time to suss us out.

However, after the introductions, by the time we've done some lifting, and started inviting some of their guys up to do some lifting, they usually relax a bit and we end up having a good laugh with them.

A number of times, we also did evening meetings on the base for soldiers and their wives, or even families. Those meetings were more relaxed. We did our usual thing – introduced ourselves, got some of the guys up for a bench press competition, did some lifting ourselves, gave our testimonies, and told them about God's power to save every single person from their sin. Having the families there made it different. We had a lot of fun, and we also saw quite a number of people touched by God over the years.

It was one of the evening meetings, where families could come, that I remember seeing a couple of quite distressed men. The padre told us it can go either way, with the trauma. Some of them cover it up with drink. But others seek spiritual help. To be honest, you could see the trauma in some of their faces. They came along to the meeting with their wives, and our hearts went out to them.

Arthur

Ian and I went to Group Strike Command at RAF Marham in Norfolk – one of the RAF's main operating bases. We went there in 2003 when they were taking off from there to attack Iraq. I remember one of the visual signs that they were actively at war was that the group commander had a set of overalls on. We did a social with them as well as a proper meeting. So that felt a significant time, because we were actually at war, and we were talking to guys who were flying out there.

Ian

In the prisons, we're constantly talking about turning from violence. We're saying, 'Turn from that darkness. Turn from your sin.' We tell our own stories, about realising that the lives of violence we were leading were wrong, and how we stopped all that when we started understanding Jesus and God, the way of love and peace.

In the army, that's a different thing altogether. They aren't reforming people, they're creating warriors. You're standing in front of people who are preparing to go out to a warzone. Whether they're in active service or a peacekeeping role, they might have to use physical force. They might have to take someone's life, or inflict an injury.

People don't even realise because there isn't war on our shores, that the army are constantly engaged in conflicts around the world. They will have been out to the Middle East, been involved with Ukraine, or Syria, Afghanistan, Somalia, working with the UN, or with the Americans. A lot of people won't be aware of that. But it's their reality. They are trained to put their lives on the line.

I don't think it's any accident that the chaplain has always had a significant role in the Armed Forces. These guys are dealing with life and death on a regular basis. Most of them will have lost a friend or brother at some point. They can't get away with not thinking about spiritual realities in that lifestyle. They don't get to sit at home with TV dinners denying the reality of pain, evil, death or hell. They are right there in it.

I remember a visit we did during one of the wars in the Middle East – probably the later stages of the Iraq War. Some of the lads had literally just come back from conflict, earlier that day. That really affected my mind. I was thinking, 'Yesterday these boys were being shot at, or had the potential of losing their lives – and everyone in England is cracking on as normal, not a clue.'

Arthur

Another of the times we went to Germany, we were address-
ing guys who had just come back from Afghanistan. That was
pretty sobering.

At the same time, some others there were about to go off on
a mission, so that was a really different feel – a sense of excite-
ment and adventure, going together as a team.

We nearly had a chance of going to Afghanistan ourselves
once – there was a visit in the pipeline, but then apparently
some celebrity went out there and messed things up, so they
blocked civilians from the foreign bases.

Ian

One particular guy came up after that meeting with the soldiers who had just got back from Afghanistan. I think he was
a sergeant – probably in his late thirties – and he had tears in
his eyes. The meeting had affected him. I don't know how – he
didn't say – he just said, 'Thank you for coming, and saying
what you said.'

You could tell from looking at him that he was a proper
bloke, who'd seen life and death, maybe even been involved
in it. He was visibly moved, and you could see that God was
working in him. Seeds had been sown.

In the army, you are close up to life and death. Arf and I
have been close to death too. Arthur has tried to take his own
life. I have had one of my best friends shot down and die right
in front of my eyes.

I'm not saying we know what it's like to serve in the forces,
but I do think we have some kind of understanding. We have

that urgency – we need to tell people this message, because who knows what life will bring, and when they will need it, or when it will be too late.

I think soldiers can see in us that we're not coming from a blasé, comfortable life, where we've always been fine and we don't understand people who are not fine. I think we have some authenticity, which men in the Armed Forces can detect, and it helps them trust us a bit, and helps us relate to them.

But that's nothing in itself. The reason we've carried on doing what we're doing, and the reason why people keep inviting us back, is because we're grounded in the gospel. We always come back to the lostness of human beings, and the saving grace of God through the cross of Jesus Christ. You can have a nice time with a guy who understands a bit how you feel – but that guy can't rescue you from the darkness inside. Only God can.

Arthur

We've had some very serious moments with the Armed Forces, but we also get invited for some very memorable occasions that it's a privilege to be a part of.

Down in Torpoint, Cornwall, there's a naval training centre – HMS Raleigh. It's been a training centre for hundreds of years. There was a minister here in Cornwall, who got us to go speak in Yeovil at the air base. After we spoke at Yeovil, the guy in charge there put us in touch with a friend of his who was a submariner leading the training centre in Torpoint. That's how we first got invited, and now it's a regular thing.

They have a ten-week training programme at Torpoint, so it's a ten-week turnover of around six or seven hundred people – men and women – who have recently joined the navy.

The navy's pretty different from the army. It's a whole different lifestyle, so there's a different headspace too. A lot of people there are doing medical stuff, coming out from university. And there are far more women than in the army. It's a real mix. Some of them are quite raw – they have joined up through becoming homeless – or for the older ones, life hasn't turned out how they wanted, and they've decided to join the navy. And of course, they're all going to spend months and months living on this ship together, so you've got this unique atmosphere, and these hundreds of people who are probably never going to be at a church.

We do the same thing as ever – lift some weights, give some testimonies, share the gospel. We've done that a couple of times a year with different chaplains, which is good because one chaplain recommends us to the next chaplain, and so on.

They always get us in on the day that a section is completing their training. It's basically a chapel service, but it's the celebration of finishing their training, so it turns into a bit of a jamboree. The chaplain will put some worship songs on, and they really go for it on the singing. They especially love the one about the lighthouse[1] – masses of them singing it at the tops of their voices.

I don't know if they know what they're singing, but they get right into it. They're pretty boisterous. They're always happy to come and join in the competition we have with the weights. But they also listen well when we're talking. The atmosphere is fun. It's very different from when you're with armies who are in active service. With these navy events, we're building into the lads and girls at an early stage in their career.

The other big occasion that sticks out is the Royal Fusiliers up in Edinburgh with Dave Jeal. We met Dave when he was a chaplain in HMP Bristol, and we stayed in touch. Then he joined the Marines as their chaplain. You have to be fully part of the army to be a chaplain – you don't just come in sideways and sit on a cushion. He was trained with the 40 Commando Royal Marines and became chaplain. After that, he was chaplain to 2nd Battalion, Royal Regiment of Scotland.

Dave invited us to go up to Scotland. This was in 2023, and it was me and Ian. The whole battalion was there, hundreds of men – everyone from the lowest soldier to the top commander.

Dave led a Christmas service. He gave a great interpretation of the Christmas story. Then we got up to speak. We didn't do any weights – we had decided not to try to fly our kit up to Scotland – but we both gave our testimony and Ian came off the back of Dave's Christmas talk, and gave the gospel in that context.

We did have a bit of a think about how to give a gospel message in that scenario. The last thing you want to do is come across sanctimonious. It's a special occasion, but some of those guys will have been in a warzone recently, and there will be a lot of conflict going on inside them.

We have nothing to offer as human beings. Nothing at all. But we do have this amazing treasure, which is the Word of God and the cross of Jesus, which is the power to save.

We went and had Christmas dinner with them all after the service. It was fantastic – a real spectacle. The officers went up to the dinner hall first, stood outside, all dressed in their kilts, to form a sort of welcoming party for the soldiers, then there was a piped band – proper bagpipes – which led the soldiers up to this enormous dining hall. They all processed in, and the officers served them their dinner. It was all very grand, and a massive privilege to be part of.

There were some promotions, and awards given out. The senior officer who was doing the speeches and presentations, a couple of times, picked up on what we had said about choices – about how we had made a choice to follow Jesus Christ. I thought that was interesting, that he picked up on something we said, that resonated with him, and used it in speaking to his soldiers.

Ian

Back in Germany once, I was sitting with the commander in his office after one of our presentations, because he wanted to discuss what we'd said. He was pulling things out of our talk that he wanted to ask about, and writing them up on a whiteboard under a heading that said 'Themes'. I remember thinking, 'Wow! I didn't even know we talked about themes!'

The military mind is different to yours or mine, and to be honest, I couldn't fathom it! But how amazing that he wanted to talk with us, and look into some of those things in more detail. That's the Word of God at work.

Arthur

I'm not questioning politics, war, or Armed Forces. I wouldn't go to war, but I'll be there for anyone who wants to be prayed for, or who wants to hear the gospel. I pray regularly with a friend whose son is in the army, and I pray for that lad. I sometimes meet up with him, when he's home.

We want peace, and when Jesus returns, there will be peace. But if we have the chance to stand in front of a load of guys to tell them about our lives and about the gospel, the week before, or the day before they are off to a warzone, we will be there.

So we have been sent to speak for Christ. It is like God is calling to people through us. We speak for Christ when we beg you to be at peace with God.

2 Cor. 5:20, ERV

Chapter Seven

From New York to Felixstowe

> Now he who plants and he who waters are one, and each
> one will receive his own reward according to his own
> labor. For we are God's fellow workers . . .
>
> *1 Cor. 3:8–9a, NKJV*

Ian

Something happened when we were out in New York.

It was 1999, so we were three or four years into the ministry. It was a spiritual watershed, if you like, and it had a lasting impact on Tough Talk's identity. That was the point where we went from a load of big lumps who bowled up however you like in whatever we were wearing, to being more of a team, organising ourselves, having a little bit of discipline. And we felt God's blessing like we hadn't before.

It was a pretty large-scale affair, that first New York trip. We took a big team. About eight of us Tough Talk guys went, but also quite a few of our wives, and some sons and daughters. Arthur had his wife, Jacqui, there, plus his kids, Emma and James, who must have been in their early twenties – Emma spoke and gave her testimony at one of the schools we visited. Then the church we were with took singers, and we also had people who were there to pray.

We'd been at it for a few years, but we hadn't seen a lot of people responding in the meetings to commit their lives to God. There were some, but not a lot. And then when we went to New York the first time, it all started – from the very first meeting. We started seeing incredible responses to the challenge, the altar call.

I remember one meeting. It was in a Hispanic church, and we had the interpreter, though a lot of them did speak English anyway. When we'd done the weights, heard the testimonies, and I'd preached the gospel, I gave an altar call, saying, 'If you want to commit your life to Jesus, then come forward to the front and we will pray for you.'

Well, they all started coming forward. Literally, all of them. Even people who were in the choir were coming forward to respond to Christ. It was such a wholesale response, I thought they'd misunderstood. I was clarifying myself through the microphone, saying, 'Hang on, what I'm asking is, if you're repenting of your sins, and deciding to trust in Jesus as your Lord and Saviour – if you realise you don't know him, you're lost and you need to be born again – then come forward and we'll pray for you.' And they carried on coming. People were even getting up out of the worship band to come forward and commit themselves. It was madness!

I thought, 'Maybe it's because they're Hispanic – maybe it's the culture – that South American vibe.'

Then we spoke at another church – Christ's Tabernacle in Queens – and we had hundreds of people come forward – literally hundreds. I thought, 'Wow, this is incredible. I've never seen so many people respond to the gospel. Maybe it's because they're Americans. Maybe it's the culture.' But it was the power of God. God was just showing up and using what we were doing and saying to touch people. It was amazing.

When people are flocking forward – when the really big stuff happens – that's when you absolutely know that it's really very little to do with you. That's the Lord calling people, and working in their lives. It's the Holy Spirit. And what a privilege to be part of it.

Arthur

One of the churches out in New York had a laugh with us. The guy up front started the meeting by saying, 'Stand up if you're a bloke.'

Well, we thought that was a bit odd. I wondered where he was going with it, to be honest. There was a congregation of a few hundred, and a lot of them were men. But we stood up, obediently.

Then we realised that the American host and audience were roaring with laughter, and we – Ian, me and the other Tough Talk guys – were the only ones standing up. Because of course only British people use the word 'bloke', so we were the only ones who'd stood up. They loved that. They had a real laugh.

Ian

At the end of that visit, part of me was still putting it down to something cultural. Maybe it was their love of our British accents, or something like that. But when we came back from the USA, the responses continued in this country in a significant way.

We came back and did a meeting in Manchester with the World Wide Message Tribe.[1] The Message Trust had hired out a big theatre hall that took three, four, maybe five thousand people – mostly young. I was preaching the same gospel message: 'We've all sinned before a holy God. We've all made mistakes. None of us are perfect. Now is the time to get right with God.' I've often used that kind of summary, based on the Romans Road to salvation,[2] as it's known.

I gave a call, and these kids were flocking forward to commit their lives to Christ. I've never seen so many young people come forward to respond to the gospel. It was breathtaking. It was a major moment of anointing on us, and on all the people that had organised the mission. Ever since that day, I get people telling me, 'I gave my life at that meeting.' They are often pastors, or youth leaders. Sometimes I meet them at an event, or they contact us to book us for something, and they say, 'I saw you at that event, and I responded that day,' and they're still living for Jesus.

We went on an open-air outreach somewhere in the UK soon after the New York trip, and without really planning it, we went into a sports shop and bought a load of matching tracksuits. That was an important step, although it happened spontaneously.

You might think it was just a style or superficial thing, but actually it was about building up this sense of team. It embodied the sense that we were all in it together, with a shared purpose.

I used to run a complicated whiteboard in the office, to get everyone signing up to the events they could come to. I'd be on the phone:

'Alan, can you do Welsh prisons, on the last Thursday in April?'

'Joe, are you free the bank holiday weekend? We're doing a beach mission.'

I'd be ticking them off and plotting who could do what. Then someone would ring me and be like, 'Ian, I can't do that school visit in Liverpool after all', or, 'Mate, I can do some of it – I can do the Saturday, but not the Sunday.' I sometimes think I was doing almost as much admin as I was evangelism in those early years.

I remember rocking up at Highpoint prison in 1994 with a whole bunch of crazy-looking fellas. We had some East End gangsters, an ex-terrorist, a thief. We took a load of people everywhere in those days. We would have a whole row of Tough Talk men sitting on the front bench. If it was a church or youth event, we would take singers with us as well.

We've done our presentation in football stadiums and festivals. We've done outreach at Alton Towers. In these big arenas, you do need a bigger team – four or five guys up on stage to capture the attention of a big crowd in a big space.

We still do some really large-scale events. On Good Friday in 2022, we did Churches Together in Chelmsford, Essex. The whole High Street was packed with people. They'd set up a big stage in an open part of the High Street, and there were hundreds of people. I didn't even know there were that many churches in Chelmsford! It was massive.

If it's on that scale, I'll get a few more people together for a bigger impact. But otherwise, these days, I'm really happy just being me and Arf, or me and Joe, or me, Arf and Joe. It's about the commitment, the willingness. It's just such a pleasure to get on with it and tell people about Jesus, which is what I can do with Arf and Joe. But back in those early days, there was a whole crew of us.

I had a guy called Andy, a boxer with an incredible conversion and healing from addiction. He lived in Wolverhampton. He contacted me and said he was interested in working with us. I thought I'd put the onus on him, sort of test out his willingness, so I said, 'Well, we have a prayer meeting on Tuesdays, down here in east London, if you want to come along?'

And he did. He drove down from the Midlands, and we prayed and had coffee. After that, we took him into prisons, got him speaking and testifying. He was great. He did a whole load of events with us, and now he has his own ministry, called Jesus In My Corner Ministry.[3] He goes out sharing his testimony, and he's brought out a book telling his story.[4] He was a great guy to work with. I felt at the time that he wouldn't necessarily be with us for long, but he really gave it his all while he worked with us. There are certain seasons where things happen a certain way, but they don't have to last for ever.

Arthur

Another character who worked with us in the early days sometimes trained at the same gym as me, and he'd always be praying for people. He was a big personality, and loud, but he was loud about the Lord. I would walk in the gym and he'd call me over to pray for some lad's earache, or stomach trouble, or something like that. He wouldn't let me get on with training till I'd prayed with him. It happened in the changing rooms too. Sometimes he was so keen to pray for people that he forgot to get dressed properly first. I loved his heart. He was proper passionate about Jesus. Still is, I believe.

Lifting the Darkness

Ian

Simon joined us later on, around 2002 or 2003, and was with us about nine years. He had a great story. He's a big guy – about 6ft 4in. He was an ex-copper turned thief, turned Christian.[5] He was a great member of the team. He's also in his own ministry now and still loves the Lord.[6] He puts on men's breakfasts and things like that.

In fact, when he was with us, we had conversations about Tough Talk setting up more men's events, but in the end, I really felt that our ministry needed to be focused on preaching the gospel, and leave the event organising to other people. So, Simon was really committed while he was with Tough Talk, then he felt led to go down that different road, so off he went, and that's great. I love that.

There was another guy with us – Adam. He was an ex-thief too, who'd come to faith, and he was dangerous, in a number of ways. He's still associated with us, actually – I still take him out with us every so often. Adam was with me before I met Arthur, so he's one of our longest-standing associates.

I'd been asked to speak at a men's dinner event one time, and I'd lined up two Tough Talk guys to come with me – one to give a testimony, and the other one to help me change the weights on the bar, and do the spotting – which is a safety thing – keeping an eye and being ready to take the weight if the person lifting suddenly tires or makes a mistake.

So, I invited these two guys, but one of them had blown me out. I was sitting in church, and I saw Adam. I'd only spoken to Adam very briefly before. He was a smallish fella with a skinhead, and he looked like a little tearaway. I went over and said, 'Adam, you've got a van, haven't you? Do you want to come out with me this weekend and help me with the weights and stuff?'

'Yeah,' says Adam.

So I asked, 'Do you want to give a testimony?'

'No,' says Adam. 'I never wanna speak.'

I said, 'That's fine.'

So, the plan was, I'd do the introduction, then I'd do some lifting, the other Tough Talk guy would give his testimony, then I'd wrap up with the gospel. Adam would be setting the weights up, adding to the load in between my lifting, and spotting for me. But when the other guy came to do his testimony, he stood up, stuttered a couple of times, then said, 'I don't know what to say!' and just completely dried up.

Everyone was looking at us, wondering what was going to happen next. I'd heard the guy give his testimony before, with no issues, so I don't know what happened that time. I was all kitted out in my lifting belt and I just thought on my feet. I jumped up to the mic, and said, 'Please give him a big clap, guys. It's so raw, his story – he's just got overwhelmed, he's a bit speechless tonight. Give him a clap!'

And everyone's like, 'Aah, poor fella,' and I continued, 'But don't worry, we've got Adam here! Adam, come up here and tell everyone what Jesus has done for you!'

Adam stands up, absolutely astonished, but he does it – he tells his story about how he'd been a thief, and then he'd begun to come to faith by reading the Jehovah's Witnesses' Bible in his little bedsit, while smoking weed. Then a little booklet came through his door about Christianity, and he read that and made a commitment.

He hadn't ever spoken about it in public, but to his credit, he just got up and said his piece. I love that about him.

He's not the world's greatest public speaker, but he's bold and he's reliable. If I ask him to share his story, or preach on the streets, he'll do it. He'll do his five-minute story, starting with 'My name's Adam' and ending with the gospel.

Adam was great to work with, but occasionally he was also a hilarious disaster.

We were doing an outreach on the streets once. We'd been doing a deadlift, and we'd gone all the way up the weights. All of them were on the bar, and the bar was on the floor – about 180kg weights on a 20kg bar, sitting on the street. And of course, we normally dismantle it all – slide the weights off the bar, take everything separately back to the van. But I'd turned my back to talk to someone, and Adam thought to himself, 'It'll be quicker if I just roll this down the High Street . . . '

Some sort of shout made me look round, and Adam, having started rolling the powerlifting bar down the road, had lost control of it. The bar was rolling down the street! People were scattering out of the way, flying all over the place! Adam was pegging it, trying to catch up with the bar as it tumbled down the High Street with 180kg of metal on it. Thankfully, it smashed into a wall, and everyone was OK. Once we knew nobody had got injured, it was absolutely hilarious.

Another time, there was a tent meeting we were in – a massive circus tent sort of affair, with quite a lot of people; a decent sized set-up. Again, instead of dismantling the bar at the end, and transporting the weights and the bar separately like you would normally do, Adam picked the whole thing up, and stuck it on his shoulders. Then he started walking from the platform, down the aisle of the tent, towards the back exit.

What Adam couldn't see was that the bar – which of course is pretty wide – had snagged on something as he came down from the front platform, and basically the whole contents of the tent were coming down and dragging along behind Adam as he went – wires, lighting, cables, even the tent itself started unravelling and following him down the aisle!

We started calling him our Health and Safety Officer in the end. He was a great member of the team and he made us laugh. He was a builder. He would come haring round the corner a bit late and jump out of the van, going, 'Sorry I'm late!' He'd start unpacking the weights, and his hands would be bleeding or something, and he'd go, 'Sorry I'm late, I was on the building site, and I've cut my hands, and then I went to the wrong church, but I'm 'ere now!' And he'd start unpacking the weights with his hands bleeding all over the place, or whatever it was. You had to smile, really. We had some hilarious times with Adam.

Arthur

Another time, we were doing an evangelistic event in Great Yarmouth, on the east coast, and Adam was late again. We were in the church, the service had just started, and no sign of Adam, so we rang him up, and he said, 'I'm outside the church!' And I was like, 'No, you're not outside the church, Adam, because we're inside the church right now, and we can see that you're not outside it!'

Turned out, Adam was in Felixstowe. He was two hours down the coast from where he should be, and he'd got all our weights!

Ian

Bless him. He got married, he's got some kids, he loves the Lord, he's still part of Tough Talk, still does events with us. I took him last year to some of the Teen Challenge chapel services that I do, in fact, and he does a bit of street outreach with us sometimes as well.

I know his capabilities. He wouldn't be intimidated to stand in front of hundreds of people on the street, or come out at night with me. Even when I've done nightclub-type outreach at night, with people swearing and shouting at him, he carries on. He says his piece. Then I know that when he stops, he stops. No messing about with Adam. I know exactly how much he's got in him. He's great at helping with the weights, but he's not a lifter as such – he's a fairly small fella, actually – which helped with being a thief, of course!

We were speaking at a church in the East End once, and we were sitting there, waiting to be asked on to the platform, and Adam was looking around a bit at the church. Then he leaned over and whispered in my ear,

'I've been here before.'

'Have you?' I said.

'Yeah,' he said. 'I broke in on a Sunday night and stole the offering!'

> The one who plants and the one who waters have the same purpose. And each one will be rewarded for his own work. We are workers together for God . . .
>
> *1 Cor. 3:8–9, ERV*

Chapter Eight

Under the Flyover

Let this mind be in you which was also in Christ
Jesus, who, being in the form of God, did not consider
it robbery to be equal with God, but made Himself of no
reputation, taking the form of a bondservant, and coming
in the likeness of men. And being found in appearance as
a man, He humbled Himself and became obedient to the
point of death, even the death of the cross.

Phil. 2:5–8, NKJV

Arthur

In everything, we go by invitation. Where we're invited, we
go. It might be Manchester City stadium full of thousands
of people. It might be a grotty backstreet in Soho, with a few
down-at-heel blokes looking for something to eat and a little
bit of hope. God's not a snob, so we can't be either.

Ian

When you go around the country and get invited to drug
rehabs and homeless projects and things like that, you realise

the church is very active. The church is feeding and cleaning and washing and helping and ministering to people. It's been quite an eye-opener.

I'd say the church engages more in social action than in evangelism. So we're called in to do the evangelistic slots.

One organisation we've both worked with a lot is London City Mission (LCM).[1] I've been working with them for about twenty years. They run practical projects around the capital, but always with the aim of sharing Jesus as well as meeting physical needs. Typically, they will operate in a church, a community centre, or homeless facility. The guys will have some food, they can get a shower, maybe pick up a blanket, but there is always a 'God Slot' as well. Sometimes, that actually happens before anything else, so it's like, 'Yes, you can come and get food and necessities, but you have to sit through the God Slot first!'

I seldom do weights at these sorts of things. It's more just a presentation of testimony and the gospel message. Increasingly in London, you have interpreters working with you, for the people who have a different first language.

The response is very positive. These are generally people on the lowest rung of the social ladder – people whom life has failed. They've not got many pretences. They know they've messed up, and they know they can't fix themselves. Some will be sleeping rough, some in shelters or temporary accommodation, just coming in for breakfast. Some are desperate to get out of their situation, and others seem quite resigned to it. Occasionally, someone will come up and ask for prayer. Others might want to drink and forget.

Last time I was down there, there was a man sitting looking through a Bible, and we got chatting. He was telling me about the hard times he'd come to, and how it had happened. It made me realise that this can happen to anyone – you're only a couple of pay cheques away from it, to be honest, especially if you haven't got family and support around you. We prayed together and it was very much a two-way thing. He was praying and ministering to me, as well as me to him.

It's very humbling, because you go in thinking, this is sort of a different type of person to me. I mean, you don't intentionally think, 'I'm better than these people,' but in the back of your mind, maybe you elevate yourself a bit, and look at them as poor desperate souls less fortunate than yourself. And then when you are with them, you realise, 'Hey, these guys are just like me, with slightly different circumstances.'

We quote that verse from Romans so often – 'all have sinned and fall short of the glory of God' (Rom. 3:23, NKJV) – then sometimes the same verse comes around and bites us in the backside! We've all messed up. Before Jesus, no one in the world – inside or outside the Church – is better than anyone else. Either you've got to answer for not living up to his holy standards, or you stand there washed in his blood, living under his forgiveness and justification in God's eyes. It's nothing to do with yourself at all, but living right with God through his free gift of grace through Jesus Christ.

When I was a young man, around 21, I found myself homeless for a little while. I was couch surfing. I never had to sleep rough, thankfully, but I slept on a lot of floors. Then I started sneaking into the gym where I was working, and sleeping on the floor there – until I got found out. That wasn't too bad – I even had a shower in the morning after sleeping there; those were the days before you had CCTV cameras everywhere. So, I had a bit of a feel for how circumstances can take you down, and it's not easy to get up again.

There was another guy I spoke with many years before in Soho. We were talking at a Christian feeding station place, around the back of a church there. He started quoting Philippians to me. 'The reason I love Jesus,' he said, 'is because, "being in very nature God, [he] did not consider equality with God something to be used to his own advantage; rather, he made himself nothing by taking the very nature of a servant, being made in human likeness. And being found in appearance as a man, he humbled himself by becoming obedient to death – even death on a cross!"[2] See how much Jesus loves me!' he said.

Arthur

You might remember when Terry Wogan hosted Radio 2 in the mornings years ago? I remember him playing a piece of music that was a homeless man singing on the street, 'Jesus loves me, this I know, For the Bible tells me so'[3] and he was absolutely pitch perfect. Somehow Terry Wogan had heard this guy, recorded it and played it on his programme, because it was utterly beautiful. It was more than just musical, there was a deep spiritual sincerity to it.

Somehow, the lowliest people can have a knowledge of God, of the Scriptures, and there's no real rhyme or reason for why they're homeless – it's not necessarily about being a good person or a bad person.

We can get the impression that the Lord loves you if you're in a good place in life and have a big lovely house. Well, that's not the case, is it?

Ian

There's a church that Joe and I have worked with over the years – North Point Church Coventry, it's called. They provide food for homeless people, under a flyover in the city.

We'll usually pick up a guy from their church, and go ahead of their vans that bring the food and other provisions. We'll pull up in our truck, and if we sit there for a few minutes, we start to see people coming towards the place, milling around, and soon there are fifty, sixty people, then more – maybe a hundred or even two hundred people, gathering under this dark, noisy, urban flyover. It's a strange sight.

The first time I did it, I said to the guy from the church, 'Who are these people?'

He said, 'This is who we're feeding.'

What you see next is a load of vans pulling up, and these guys from the church jump out and start unpacking. Foldable tables. Tureens of soup. Piles of blankets. Then a PA system with some speakers. I remember them saying to us, one of the first times we did it, 'What we're going to do is put up a PA for you here, and I want you to do the weights, and then preach the gospel. Give it some welly, give it everything, no need to hold back – heaven, hell, come forward if you want prayer, prayer for healing, sickness, disease, you know, it's all good.'

It's a crazy thing, because it looks so random – gathering under this flyover with the traffic rumbling overhead and all around you. It's all very shadowy under there, so you see all these figures gathering and waiting on a big triangle of concrete. It's mainly men, but there are some women and children too, and they gather up to an hour beforehand.

It's one of the wilder ones I've done – it's less contained than other venues, so you don't really feel in control in any way!

So, we got out the weights. We set up the bench and we did a few bench presses, which they quite liked, but you could tell they were really there for the food. So, we cut to the chase, and preached the gospel. And people were listening, they were coming forward for prayer as well. Then, after they'd eaten, some of the men were coming forward to listen to us, and I remember in the end, me and Joe sitting on our bench, just chatting about Jesus with a load of these guys. We were answering their questions and explaining our faith.

In these kinds of scenarios, people give us attention, and they respond. Similarly to when we go into prisons, these people know they are sinners, they know they are in a mess. They are already looking for hope, they are looking for a saviour. Whereas when you go into an affluent businessmen's dinner, it can be like banging your head against a brick wall. How do you convince that person who is successful, wealthy and self-sufficient that they are a sinner, that they will stand before a holy God and be found wanting, and that they need God's forgiveness? It's very different.

A church I did just before lockdown had a brilliant idea. They had started laying on an alternative service after the main services, because generally these guys don't want to come into the main church – they find it intimidating. But together, in their own company, they really love the Lord. There are a number of small churches now specifically catering to people on the streets, making church for them where they can feel like they belong.

There's one in Norwich that we know well, and another one I do is called Jumping Jacks in Glasgow.[4] It's a church in a pub – an old pub that someone got shot in and died, and they closed the pub. That was back in the eighties or nineties. Then a Christian couple had a vision that the Lord was going to bring the down-and-outs into this pub, and they were going to do church.

Every Friday night, they set it up. They bring in some benches. They've got a big cross on the wall, and posters with Scripture on them. They serve coffee, tea and biscuits from the old bar, and they welcome people in. You get a mixture of drug addicts, Christians, characters off the street, all sorts. Some have come to faith, some haven't, some are right on the edge of all sorts of things.

When they're all in, they get the piano open and start singing and praising Jesus. They love all the old hymns there and they belt them out – they really make a big racket. 'I Stand Amazed',[5] 'It is Well',[6] 'How Great Thou Art'[7] – that kind of thing. The presence of God is among those people more than any other church I've ever been in. The Holy Spirit is there, full on. They all prophesy,[8] they speak in tongues, they're on fire, and they like it loud and rough. They want you to be loud and rough, too, and to be honest, I've sat there, more than anywhere, and thought, 'I'm not worthy for the task, Lord – what can I bring?' Because it's just so humbling to be with people who humanly have nothing – some of them don't know where they're going next, or what they're going to do when church finishes – but spiritually, they have this incredible treasure and the most amazing connection with God.

There's a woman there who I have chatted to, whose mum was an alcoholic. She became an alcoholic too, but she came to faith in God, and her life has been turned around. Now she's a prison officer. She loves the Lord. Then her mum became a Christian too. They both got set free from alcohol addiction, through going to Jumping Jacks. I ended up going into the prison she works at – a female prison – and preaching there too.

I think what I see in these places is the church at its best – providing for material needs, but realising that our spiritual status is still more important. Matthew 16:26 says, 'what profit is it to a man if he gains the whole world, and loses his own soul?' (NKJV).

That is the essence of our work as evangelists. We are there to point people towards the one who can save your very soul.

Arthur

Certain individuals within the church get it, working with these kinds of guys. They can stink of alcohol, and yet they're talking about Jesus – that messes with what you expect a Christian to be like. So, there are some people who get it, and some who don't.

The ones who are stuck trying to work out the rights and wrongs of it all are the people who struggle most to relate to troubled individuals. But others just go with the randomness. They can see that Jesus' love surfaces in the most unexpected places and people.

Ian

One place I preach at very regularly is Teen Challenge (London),[9] which is now based in a large old house – Drayton Hall – outside Norwich.[10] This is a drug rehab centre – a residential place – that was started by my pastor, Steve Derbyshire, and a man called Javier Lester. It's part of the international Teen Challenge movement, which was originally begun by David Wilkerson, the Christian evangelist who wrote *The Cross and the Switchblade*.[11]

It's like an eighteen-month Christian boot camp to kick addiction. It's tough. Lots of discipline and rules. Looking after your room, making your bed, learning to cook, all that. It's a very structured programme. It's in modules, so if something goes wrong, you slip back and have to repeat that module, but you can still carry on. There's a second-hand furniture business that helps support the organisation from its profits, and where the men on the programme can help out. They've opened up a coffee shop too, where some of the guys work. So there's lots going on.

There are always some people who run after a week or so, but for those that stick it out, the success rate is incredibly high. And faith is an integral, non-optional part of it.

I do the service at the chapel there once a month on a Saturday. I generally won't have a long message prepared. I'll have had a think and a pray, and I'll go with what the Holy Spirit seems to be saying, because he knows what's going on in the guys who are there. Some of these men are on the edge, thinking of leaving – and they need to hear a message from God.

What I mostly see there are men who have come to their senses, and realised that they have a life they never wanted. They've suddenly thought, 'I'm 30 years old and I can't remember the last ten years of my life.' The younger they are, the more they still have a belief that they can get through it themselves, but as they get older, they realise they need help.

The worship with these guys can be very powerful, because it's so real. They are seeking after God, they have an openness, an eagerness, and no complacency, because they know what life is like. I'd go there any Sunday pretty much, rather than a 'normal' church. It's amazing how the programme builds faith alongside getting people off their addictions. The way they teach about the gospel is better than most churches, in my experience.

There are some great stories coming out of Teen Challenge. There's a guy we've met who had been a heroin addict, funding his habit through crime, in and out of prison for years. He got sent to Teen Challenge, became a Christian and kicked it all. Now he's working as a case worker and mentor in rehabilitation.

They know it's Christianity which gets them through it and off the drugs. At one point, the organisation was getting some funding from the council. Then the council said they would only keep the funding going if Teen Challenge toned the God stuff down, but they said no. They turned down the funding. They knew that if you take that bit away, it's not going to work. God is the key.

The Bible says, 'Salvation belongs to our God' (Rev. 7:10, NKJV).

You can make things a bit better through your own efforts, and you can change a lot about your life with good friends, professional help, and all that. But what we all really need is to be saved from the darkness within us. And only God can do that. That's the business he's in.

Arthur

We did a drug rehab in New York and they had had an audit done by the local authority. The way they told it to us, the guy doing the audit couldn't work out why the Christian rehab had such an amazing success rate, while the statutory services weren't getting that. In the end, they said, he wrote in his report that the only way he could explain the difference was 'the Jesus factor'. And he left it at that.

In your life together, think the way Christ Jesus thought. He was like God in every way, but he did not think that his being equal with God was something to use for his own benefit. Instead, he gave up everything, even his place with God. He accepted the role of a servant, appearing in human form. During his life as a man, he humbled himself by being fully obedient to God, even when that caused his death – death on a cross.

Phil. 2:5-8, ERV

Chapter Nine

Wolves, Snakes and Doves

Behold, I send you out as sheep in the midst of wolves.
Therefore be wise as serpents and harmless as doves.

Matt. 10:16, NKJV

Ian

The media coverage all started with the *Sunday Telegraph*. I think it was August 2001. They came to interview Arthur, Steve and me. Then a load of other media outlets got hold of the story – as they do – and we got in all sorts of newspapers, news programmes, radio features and on the telly. I think at one stage we were on telly every week for about a month and a half. We were on pretty much every television channel: BBC, Channel 4, Channel 5, Sunday morning programmes, lots of Christian TV. Our story just captured people's imagination. For a while.

Arthur

Even today, I'm not sure how it all came about, or why we got so much publicity all of a sudden. It was a centre-page spread in the *Telegraph* of the three of us. Loads of my old weightlifting mates saw that. Then all this TV stuff. I think Ian and I did a couple of TV things on our own, but predominantly it was all of Tough Talk – they liked to have a big group of us fellas. They loved the hardman-to-religion angle.

Ian

It was quite funny, really. It certainly didn't go to our heads, because in between the TV, we were doing the same old events and things. We could be in a central London TV studio on Sunday morning, then by Sunday evening we'd be talking to twenty fidgeting kids at a Boy's Brigade meeting in a drafty hut.

I knew even then that it was just a season, and you make the most of the opportunities. Whether you're giving someone a cup of water,[1] because it's what the Lord has asked you to do, or if you're standing in front of 50,000 people in Manchester City stadium preaching, because it's what the Lord has asked you to do, it's all the same really, because you're doing it to the glory of God.

Arthur

With the drugs, I'd been banned from powerlifting, and I wanted to get back in – I wanted to coach again, and be part of that world. When I phoned up British Weightlifting to talk about going back after my drugs ban, I was expecting to get a proper grilling, but I phoned up John Lear, who was in charge at the time, and he said, 'I've been reading your story in the *Telegraph*, Arthur,' and he asked me when I wanted to return.

So that was a very good outcome for me. But apart from that, I don't remember being excited or thrilled, or starry-eyed at the media attention. I never thought we'd become super-stars, and there was certainly no money in it! I think I just rode the wave, and it was a good platform; it brought a lot of interest from churches and people wanting to book us. But mainly, I found it all quite puzzling.

Ian

There's a lot of people out there who want to mock Christianity, so I stayed very alert the whole time – you've got to be. I was trying to make sure we could be seen presenting the gospel in a way that didn't come over as freaky and weird.

We did a programme about what's going on in London in the evenings – it was called *London Live* or *Late London*, or *Live, Late London* – something like that. Anyway, it was going out at 11 o'clock on a Friday night and they were filming different things going on. We were sharing our story and the gospel with a youth group in south London. One of the clips was our mate Steve, in his gruff East End voice, saying, 'Christianity's not about smells and bells, it's about a relationship with Jesus Christ.' That was just perfect. Then there was a warning before the programme started, saying something like, 'This programme contains a religious theme that some viewers might find offensive.'

In actual fact, we were sandwiched between an item about a mass social event and one about an adult bondage club. I remember looking at the programme thinking, 'What on earth is going to come next!' There was this group of people promoting a bondage club, and the warning was about us talking about religion. I still can't believe that.

I think we were always a little bit on our guard. Both of us would have had some experience of media attention – me in bodybuilding and Arthur in his powerlifting – so we knew very well that you could be flavour of the month one moment, and drop out of sight the next. We also knew the power of the media to spin the story however they feel.

Early on in my bodybuilding career, I was interviewed by my local paper. I must have been in my early twenties and I'd just won my first title. They asked me loads of questions about bodybuilding – the lifestyle, the competitions, the training. One of the questions was about my diet – they said, 'What's the secret?'

So I said, 'Eggs. I eat loads of eggs'

They said, 'How do you eat them?'

I replied, 'I drink them raw. I drink raw eggs, five at a time, four times a day.'

The article came out, and turns out, I made the centre-page spread in the *Newham Recorder*! However, where I'd hoped they would have a headline about being British bodybuilding champion, instead it read: 'EGGStra-strong Ian eats 7,000 eggs a year!!' And all over the article, in between pretty much every paragraph, they put comical pictures of eggs! Even in the picture I'd posed for, they'd added eggs. It was a classic 'Archer' pose, just like Arnold Schwarzenegger used to do, with one arm tucked in, and one extended out front, to show the arm muscles. They'd put that in, but where my extended arm was pointing to, was a subheading which said, 'This is no yolk!'

I walked into the gym later that day, and my pals thought it was hilarious. They'd bought a load of copies of the newspaper and stuck up pictures of me and eggs all over the gym.

I can laugh at that now, but at the time I was pretty upset. It felt demeaning. There was nothing untrue in it, but it taught me that the media will tell the story they want to tell, in the way they want to tell it. It taught me to be wise in dealing with them.

So, in the midst of this media attention, I had *London Tonight* contact me – the local news programme. They wanted to do an item on us. We were doing a youth meeting that evening in Southend, so they sent a camera crew down. Arthur was there with me and another three guys, all dangerous-looking characters – lots of shaved heads and tattoos. We were doing this youth club. They said, 'We would like to film you praying.'

I said OK, but immediately thought, 'This could go dangerously wrong . . . ' So, I took the guys aside, and said to them, 'Look, they want to film us praying. What we're going to do is this: we'll come into a circle, and we'll bow our heads. I'm gonna pray, and you don't say anything, just keep your hands down, and just say "Amen" at the end. Don't start speaking in tongues, or screaming from the rooftops, or anything that might look crazy.'

So they filmed us, and I prayed for the kids. I just said, 'Bless the young people tonight, Lord,' and that sort of thing.

And as it turned out, that was the last clip they put in their report of us. It was on right at the end of the programme, and it was perfect. It finished with the camera panning up the arm of one of the guys. It panned up his tattooed arm, over his broad shoulder, and just as it reached his big, shaven head, this massive lump of a man gave a little nod, and quietly said, 'Amen.'

It cut back to the presenters in the studio, and there was a split second of silence. Then both presenters went, 'Wow, that was lovely. Wasn't that amazing?'

They were looking for a story and we gave it to them – *hard men, turned nice, helping and praying for young people.* Not *hard men gone a bit crazy, looking like religious lunatics indoctrinating our kids.* It's all about headline and stories. So, pray and ask God to give you wisdom, and if you're being filmed, look normal, relate to the people around you. Essentially, you're in their hands – they can edit, they can send things off in all sorts of directions. But if you give them a good story, then they won't have to go looking for a story themselves. These are really important things. As Christians in this country, too often we let ourselves look either weak, or completely spaced out.

As Jesus said, 'be as wise as serpents and harmless as doves' (Matt. 10:16, NKJV). We're being totally authentic – telling our own stories, being who we are – but we're also being wise about how people are going to interpret what we say and do.

We know that things can get twisted. We've seen Christian people or organisations really done over in the media. We ourselves have been fortunate. We've had all that coverage – press, television, all of it – and it's all been positive!

I think I enjoyed the publicity purely for the fact that we were sharing the gospel, it didn't give me anything more than that. If I was asked to go on Oprah, I'd be delighted, because it would be a great chance to share the gospel. But I wouldn't be excited about it in any other way. I don't think any of us were caught up in that, because we wouldn't be here any more if so. You're a novelty, and they will all move on to someone else pretty soon.

Arthur

It did also catapult the work into the spotlight, and open up more events for us. In 2001 we did more than 500 meetings! We used to cram loads in to the same day or weekend. We did a mission in Milton Keynes, and in just two weeks, we did more than forty presentations – five or six churches, a load of prison presentations, school visits and street work. It was crazy, but that's how we like it. Get on with it.

You can get caught up in the media-type work, but Ian and I are grounded blokes. We've both grafted, we've run our own businesses. I wouldn't call myself an intellectual, but I'm not a mug. We learned early on that we were not going to be some of these evangelists that earn thousands of dollars preaching on telly, and we're both very happy about that.

> Listen! I am sending you, and you will be like
> sheep among wolves.
> So be smart like snakes. But also be like doves
> and don't hurt anyone.
>
> *Matt. 10:16, ERV*

Chapter Ten

Lift Weights and Give God the Glory

This is a faithful saying and worthy of all acceptance,
that Christ Jesus came into the world to save sinners, of
whom I am chief. However, for this reason I obtained
mercy, that in me first Jesus Christ might show all
longsuffering, as a pattern to those who are going to
believe on Him for everlasting life.

1 Tim. 1:15–16, NKJV

Joe's story

My name is Joe Lampshire. I grew up in Essex. I came to faith
in my late teens, and around the age of 18, I started lifting
weights. Later on in life, I would be introduced to powerlifting, where I started to compete and win competitions. But at
first, it was simply the enjoyment of being strong, keeping in
shape and challenging myself to be the best I could.

At the same time, I started working in the City. I was within
the financial sector – a broker – and I lived a very hedonistic
lifestyle. I had also recently come to believe in Jesus, but at
that time, there were a lot of temptations around, and I didn't

always live up to my faith. The City lifestyle was like a bubble full of worldly pleasures – alcohol, women, ambition, success, money, adulation.

I also, stupidly, got involved in the occult. One of the things I got drawn into by friends was Ouija boards, and this ended up making me heavily oppressed and often attacked by evil spirits. I had nightmares, fears and visitations. It was horrific. Very real and very frightening.

Shortly after coming to faith, I went to a Christian holiday camp called Spring Harvest, and while worshipping I fell down on the floor screaming and cursing at everyone around me. An experienced Christian prayed for me in Jesus' name. I then remember coughing and belching and then finally being delivered, with the evil spirits coming out of my mouth.

I was totally delivered of the evil. I vowed to follow Jesus for the rest of my life. Nothing else had given me the freedom from fear, or the unconditional love I experienced then.

After that, God and lifting were the two big things in life for me. I remember sitting in St John's Church, Buckhurst Hill, and praying, 'Lord, if there is any way I can lift weights and give you the glory, then I pray it will happen.'

A few years later, while working for a small broking firm, I was in a very traditional and elite market that only brokers can enter. One of the waiters there was a Christian, and we often chatted. I remember seeing a video of Tough Talk on his desk, and he said, 'Take it, and have a watch.'

I took it back to my office in Fenchurch Street, and watched it in my lunch hour. I was inspired by what I saw – powerful men of God sharing their faith and lifting weights. I remember praying that God would somehow lead me to get involved.

I scribbled down the address from the back of the video onto a Post-it note, and promised myself to call them, but I never did and subsequently forgot all about it. Thankfully, God hadn't forgotten!

Three years later, I was training at a country club with a friend. I saw another man training. I felt like I recognised him, but couldn't think why. I asked my friend who it was.

'That's Arthur White,' he said, and I asked for an introduction.

Arthur was immediately warm and friendly, and then the Lord reminded me that he was part of Tough Talk and on the video I had watched a few years earlier. Without hesitation I said to him, 'I've been praying that I would join you guys,' and Arthur, with barely a heartbeat, said, 'As it happens, son, we've been praying for new members.'

Arthur became my spiritual godfather, and took me under his wing. He introduced me to powerlifting, and was my physical training mentor. He was 48 years old at the time and I was 25. I wanted to be like him. I was young, and I was trying to find my place and work out who I was. Little did I know, God was taking me on a journey that would radically change my life.

I was now still working in the City, but full of faith. However, I didn't really have anyone I was accountable to, so I was definitely struggling in some areas. Shortly after meeting Arthur, he introduced me to Ian McDowall, the founder of Tough Talk, and they invited me out on the streets, lifting weights and telling my testimony of being set free by Jesus Christ.

After meeting Arthur and Ian, and joining Tough Talk, I felt I needed to get more serious. Not necessarily more serious about God – I already was – but I needed to surrender more areas of my life to him. I was now in frontline ministry – there was nothing to hide behind. I had to be honest, upfront and transparent.

Ian and Arthur were brilliant. None of us were prepared to get up there and pretend everything was good when it wasn't. Sometimes I said to them, 'Lads, I'm really struggling at the moment. I need to step back for a few weeks. I'm not in the right place for this,' and they got it, they understood.

Sometimes they would say to me, 'Joe, we're not taking you out this weekend. You need to get some stuff sorted.'

And I would do that – I would spend time thinking, praying, reading my Bible and seeking God, surrendering areas in my life to God. Then I could get back on the road again.

I've always wanted to discover God as he really is, not make him what I want him to be, and the only way to do that is to get into the Word, to study the Bible.

In no way have I ever become perfect, but when I invited Jesus into my life, he changed my heart. I no longer had a desire to do all the wicked things that I used to enjoy: sleeping around, getting drunk, pornography, coarse jokes, manipulating and hurting people. Jesus truly turned my heart of stone to flesh, and placed his Spirit in me.[1]

There is a level of lifestyle authenticity that you need to have if you're going to face people – the public, prisoners, schoolkids – and say, 'Jesus changed my life, and I think you need him too.' You can do it when you're still a work in progress – which is what we all are – but I believe that if you are intentionally continuing in sinful behaviour, then you need to step away from ministry, repent of your sins and seek God's forgiveness before you get back up front. So much damage has been done over the years by pastors and leaders who have not practised what they have been preaching – leading immoral lifestyles while preaching the Bible on a Sunday morning. Anyone can fall into temptation, but – as we say in Tough Talk – there's a big difference between falling into it and swimming in it. If you fall in, get yourself out, clean yourself off, and get on with a godly life again.

Through Arthur, I discovered that I was pretty good at powerlifting. I first competed aged 27, and went on to win the East Midlands Divisional Championships in 2004. My total weight lifted meant that I qualified for the British Championships in 2005, where I won silver. That same year, I competed at the Commonwealth Championships and European Championships, where I picked up a silver and a bronze medal. In the process, I also held the British squat and total record. My best squat was 335kg. The following year, I competed at the British Championships again and won Gold in my category, breaking the British record.

So, I was working with Tough Talk in parallel with my training and competing. It was an answer to prayer, to be on the road with the lads, talking about lifting, discussing our faith and telling other people about the power of God to change lives.

There are so many stories I could tell about my years with Tough Talk – from the absolutely inspirational to the downright hilarious.

One of the most memorable highlights for me was in Queens, when I was part of the Tough Talk team visit to New York in 1999. It was a breakfast meeting in a big church. The place was full of big, powerful men. A number of us from Tough Talk had told our stories, and Ian was inviting people to respond by coming to the front if they wanted Jesus in their lives.

As Ian gave the invitation, it was like a tsunami as what seemed like hundreds of men broke out of their seats and came rushing to the front of the church – wave after wave of them. Many of them were breaking down in tears.

I looked at Arthur, watching them from the front platform, and he was properly welling up, and that set me off as well. There was this sea of hardened men running, just running forward in tears to meet God. When you know what it's like to be freed from sin, and then you see people coming forward to invite the Holy Spirit to do that same work in them, it's very moving.

When journalist Martin Saunders travelled with the team to New York the following year, he described it perfectly: 'You possibly haven't experienced the true power of the Christian message until you've seen six and a half foot of hardened gangster sobbing uncontrollably in another man's arms.'[2]

Another New York memory is from Rikers Island prison. We did a powerlifting demonstration in the gymnasium, and then gave the altar call to a room full of hardened criminals, and they all started standing up. It was pretty emotional. A female prison officer got to her feet as well – in front of the prisoners she was responsible for.

There was this beautiful sense of precious brokenness, when people who are at their wits' end realise there is hope. There was an incredible sense of the presence of God in that place. It was a great privilege to be part of it.

Equally, there have been times when something has happened and we've just had to laugh.

One day we did a street outreach in east London, and when we arrived, there was a Christian puppeteer already set up doing a puppet show. There were a few people watching him. We set up to his left, with our PA and our weights and everything, and when he had finished, we did our thing – we were noisy and upbeat and we gathered a bit of a crowd.

One member of the public took umbrage, however. He marched up to Ian, shouted in his face, and then stalked off saying he was going to call the police.

When we had finished preaching and lifting, we packed up. I was in the back of the van, waiting for Ian to start the engine, when I noticed about six police officers suddenly swarm into the space we had previously occupied. The guy who'd taken offence must have called them to get rid of the noisy Christians he had objected to.

As our van started up, I saw these officers run up, have a quick look about them for the 'noisy Christians', and notice the poor solo Christian puppeteer, who'd still got his show set up. Presumably they thought he must be the one who had been complained about. The last thing I glimpsed as we pulled away was this one guy, surrounded by police officers, getting rather more attention than he had bargained for.

Another time, in my earlier years with Tough Talk, I was under Arthur's wing, and I was doing the lifting at an open-air event. We had our bench press set up on the back of a flatbed truck, and we were running a competition for anyone who wanted to join in and lift against me.

There were two brothers, a bit younger than me, and they came to lift. They were very strong – stronger than me – and they knocked me out of the competition. I stayed on the platform, as I was helping to spot, but I remember feeling angry and embarrassed that they had both beaten me. My pride had taken a massive blow. I then remember one of the brothers attempting to bench a lot of weight to win the competition. To my shame, I didn't want him to succeed.

He failed. As the bar went down on his chest, he didn't have the strength to push it off. However, instead of lifting it straight off him, I let him struggle for a couple of seconds before helping. I wanted to emphasise his failure, I guess. But as soon as I'd lifted it clear and he was getting up, I felt what I can only describe as like a lightning bolt go through me, and God saying, 'Don't mess with my anointed.'

I was immediately shaken and very much brought back down to earth. I didn't know exactly what the words meant, but I knew what God was saying – he was telling me to get rid of my pride and arrogance against that lad who was lifting. I was reminded that we are all God's creation, and I was a lot more careful about my attitude after that.

God is a kind Father, but he's a fearsome Father too – he does rebuke his children, and I needed rebuking at that point. I'll never forget the feeling, that sense of quick, fast power on me – of God seeing right through to my grubby little heart.

I love God, but I also have so much respect for him. It is a kind of fear, but like a holy reverence, not a dread or terror. I'm not afraid that he'll stop loving me, not for a second. There's something in the Bible that I think applies to me. It says that those who have been forgiven much, love much.[3] I have had a lot of stuff forgiven in my life – some really serious issues and actions, faults and failures. So somehow, compared to a person who hasn't done the stuff I've done, I do realise how amazing God's forgiveness is, and I am so enormously grateful and thankful. I will never forget it.

I now work full-time for a small broker that provides insurance for oil and gas companies. I go out to Tough Talk events whenever I can. I'll often be out at the weekends – either just me and Ian, or with Arthur as well – and quite often I will take annual leave to take part in events or missions.

I married Denise in 2004, and apart from coming to faith, it's been the most amazing thing in my life. I call her my Earthly Rock. She keeps me grounded, she makes me whole. I've also got two children, so I have to make sure I get the balance right between spending time with the family, working to provide for them, and being out on the road.

Tough Talk has definitely changed over the years. It's kind of been refined. When I started with the guys, it was a lot more rough and ready. There was probably more ego on show, more 'bravado' and a lot of testosterone! There were more men involved, which was great, but sometimes a bit unwieldy – all these big characters coming and going.

In the later years, as we have got older, our emphasis has become more and more focused on the gospel and less on the weights. In fact, we would often prefer just to tell our stories and preach the gospel rather than take the weights with us everywhere, but for most events, the organisers like us to bring the weights as well.

God doesn't actually need me, but he has been so gracious to use me and equip me to do his will on earth at this time, with Tough Talk. I truly believe that in his divine mercy, God has used Tough Talk to minister in many places, where many people's lives have been changed. It's an amazing ministry to be involved in and an incredible answer to that prayer I made many years before Tough Talk existed, sitting in St John's,

Buckhurst Hill asking God if there was any way that I could lift weights and by doing so, give him the glory . . .

> Here is a true statement that should be accepted without question: Christ Jesus came into the world to save sinners, and I am the worst of them. But I was given mercy so that in me Christ Jesus could show that he has patience without limit. Christ showed his patience with me, the worst of all sinners. He wanted me to be an example for those who would believe in him and have eternal life.'
>
> *1 Tim. 1:15–16*, ERV

Chapter Eleven

Escaping Through the Flames

Let us hold fast the confession of our hope without
wavering, for He who promised is faithful. And let us
consider one another in order to stir up love and good
works, not forsaking the assembling of ourselves together,
as the manner of some, but exhorting one another, and so
much the more as you see the Day approaching.

Heb. 10:23–25, NKJV

Arthur

Male audiences and men's meetings have always been a big
part of Tough Talk. We naturally lend ourselves to that sort
of thing.

In the days back when Ian and I were competing and
training, the gyms were all-male environments. I worked on
a building site, then had a construction business. We both
worked on the doors, and Ian had a security business for a
while. They were all very male scenarios.

It wasn't a coincidence that prisons were one of the first
places we started going. We've also always done a lot of men's

events – breakfasts, curry nights – put on by churches, individuals, or Christian organisations. Men are a bit more likely to be interested in the weights and the hardman stories of course, and that has been a draw for a lot of blokes. But that's not the whole story. Even for guys who aren't into fitness or strength or whatever, we seem to be able to reach them.

There's something about being men talking to men, which God has really used. Men love to hear us talking honestly about life – our problems and issues as well as the good stuff.

Paul says in his letter to the Corinthians: 'I have become all things to all people so that by all possible means I might save some' (1 Cor. 9:22, NIV). I get that. Men come in all shapes, sizes and interests, but they're still men, and God does seem to have gifted us in Tough Talk with an ability to connect with all sorts of men, from dockers to brain surgeons.

Some men want to go to work, get home, talk about cars and football, have a beer and that's that. Other men are not into any kind of sport or competition, but they want to talk politics, or they like to watch cooking programmes. Whichever kinds of people we're with, we try to talk about the things they are interested in, because that's breaking down barriers. We don't change who we are, but we find ways of having common ground.

I was at a men's meeting, and a bloke spoke to me afterwards, and he said, 'Thank you very much, that was really interesting, but I'm not like you.'

'What do you mean?' I asked.

'I'm not really into weightlifting, or going to the gym,' he said. 'I don't particularly like sport, and I'm not mad on cars or football.'

So I said, 'That's alright, mate. What are you into, then?'

And he said, 'I'm a foster parent.'

It turned out, he and his wife were fostering four kids and he told me about it – what it was like, what the kids' needs were, and how he and his wife tried to meet those needs, and give the kids a stable and loving home.

I said, 'What a great testimony, and what a great man you are. You're being a father to kids who really need that.'

And you could see him sort of growing, standing taller as I encouraged him.

Ian

There's a disconnect sometimes between men's understanding of themselves, and their understanding of God, Christianity and the church. Arf and I will both testify that we had a particular impression of Christian men before we came to faith. We thought they were all wishy-washy wimps, who went around wearing socks and sandals, and that impression was initially a barrier for us.

Women and girls seem to more naturally get stuck in at church, from my experience. They take responsibility for their faith and their spiritual growth. Sometimes the church culture can feel a bit feminine as a result. I don't know why, but that is the experience.

I once had a minister get up in front of his congregation after we had done a presentation, and apologise for the amount of testosterone in church that morning. I didn't find that a particularly helpful comment, but I suppose if you're used to church being very female or feminine, and then Tough Talk comes along, you will probably notice the difference.

I'm not blaming anyone for how the church is, but I do know that God loves to see guys taking responsibility for their own spiritual lives.

I don't like seeing men who trail into church after their wives and scarper again at the end to go catch the football. I like to see men of all kinds who are interested in knowing more about God, and following his commands. It doesn't bother me whether they're into football, rugby, bodybuilding, powerlifting, chess, model-making, knitting or ballet. I think God has enabled us to speak into men's lives – to use male gatherings to bring a challenge that they wouldn't respond to in the same way if they were sitting next to their wife, or in front of their friend and his wife. With men's events, you can get under the skin in a different way.

We did a massive men's conference in Belfast, Northern Ireland, around 2003. It was called Mandate. There were at least a couple of thousand men there. People travelled from all over the UK. We had a great event that night, I remember – people were loving what we had to say, and many guys responded in some way, gave their lives, or recommitted themselves to God. But what really stuck with me was a conversation we had with a man afterwards. He had been going to commit suicide that night. He had determined that he was going to end his life, and this meeting was the last thing he would do. Then, by listening to our testimonies, he became convinced that there was a bigger picture, a purpose out there for him. He started to believe that there was a way out of the immediate, overwhelming problems that had been burying him. We had our hammers with us that time – two enormous wooden hammers about 4ft long, and you hold them in your stretched-out arms and see who can stand like that for longest. Quite a few blokes came to do the contest, and we'd had a blast. It was a real buzz.

So, you're talking to 2,000 people, having a bit of fun, throwing out seeds of faith, and you come down off the stage, and think, 'That was good,' and you're complimenting Joe on his lifting, and everyone's full of laughs, then one conversation later, and you suddenly realise that God has used you to save someone's life. Literally. The Bible says that some people 'will be saved – even though only as one escaping through the flames' (1 Cor. 3:15, NIV).

Jude says in his letter, 'Be merciful to those who doubt; save others by snatching them from the fire' (Jude 22–23).

So sometimes, you can be there when it's the last chance – the final moment when someone can respond to God.

We were very humbled that night, and it does make you think, 'I want to keep doing this, I want to keep being obedient,' because who knows how many miracles God is working through us doing our little presentation down here?

Arthur

There was another instance about five or so years ago, just before lockdown, and that was a Christian Vision for Men (CVM) meeting, where a guy had come to the meeting because something had gone wrong with a dodgy deal he'd been involved in, and some kind of gang was trying to find him. He'd tried to take refuge with a friend, but the friend had said, 'Look, I'm going away to a conference – you'd better come too.' He did, and he wasn't listening to the meeting at all, really, he was just thinking how hopeless his life was, how he was probably going to lose his life, so why shouldn't he do it himself rather than wait for someone else to do it? He had a few beers and was going to walk out of that conference and take his own life, but as he was walking to the exit, he heard Tough Talk get up and start giving testimonies. And he stopped, and listened. He didn't take his life. In fact, he gave his life to Jesus. We didn't find out till a couple of years later – he listened to our presentation, and responded to someone on the night, who scooped him up and discipled him. That was amazing. Praise God.

We did another event, in the south of England somewhere, and there was a young man who came to talk to us afterwards, to tell us that we'd spoken at that same church a number of years ago, and it had changed his life. He wasn't a Christian when he had come the first time, but he was into his training, so he'd come along to see the powerlifting. He'd been drinking before coming to the meeting, and was a bit the worse for wear, but he was a big, strong lad. Apparently, he'd won the competition on the bench press, and then had to run straight outside to be violently sick from drinking too much.

'I came back in again, though, and hung around,' he said. 'I was helping you load the van at the end, Arthur, and you said to me, "Son, you've got to sort your life out. Because you're going down the road I was going down with drink and drugs, and it'll be over in a moment. You've heard my story – it was Jesus Christ – now sort yourself out."'

That's all I said to him, apparently, then I got in the van and we drove away. But that couple of sentences was all he needed. It was all God needed, to get through to him. He sorted his life out. He investigated God. He became a Christian. He got married to a lady in his church – and there he was, standing before us two years later, clean, sober, joyful and living for the Lord.

I love how we just play our part, and God uses it in amazing ways.

Ian

The Bible says, 'There are different kinds of spiritual gifts, but they are all from the same Spirit. There are different ways to serve, but we serve the same Lord. And there are different ways that God works in people, but it is the same God who works in all of us to do everything' (1 Cor. 12:4–6, ERV).

When we're relying on the Holy Spirit, and obeying God in what he's called us to do, I think there's this beautiful shared work between us, other Christians, the person themselves and God. Someone invites them to a meeting, we say our piece, God speaks to them through our words, they respond to God, and then another Christian, or a church, picks up the baton and disciples them.

Arthur

I was so fortunate to have that guy at my church – the pastor, Vin, who originally took me under his wing and properly discipled me. His life was nothing like mine, actually. He had had a lovely upbringing, no money worries, all neat and tidy, and he'd never met a man like me in his life. But that didn't stop us having a connection – and it didn't intimidate him. We would read the Bible together, and he would teach me about it. He would explain Christianity to me, answer my questions, show me verses in the Bible that backed up the way Christians live and understand God.

Alongside that, there were very simple but really important things like setting boundaries. If we arranged to meet from 4 p.m. to 5 p.m., he was always ready to start at 4 p.m. If I was half an hour late, we still finished at 5 p.m., even if I wanted to carry on. I'd had a chaotic life, so it took me a while to get used to that rigidity, but in the end, it taught me a lot. It taught me respect for others, and their time. It taught me discipline.

Also, Vin did not disrespect me by holding back when there was something to say. Sometimes he would sit me down and go: 'You can't do that Arthur, you've got to stop that, you know where it's going to lead . . . ' He was a trained counsellor, as well as a church pastor, and he was just a very decent man who lived up to his beliefs. I was so fortunate to have someone caring for me in that way, and I knew it.

I remember getting stopped by the police once in my lorry, just for a routine check; I was on my way to see Vin. The police were checking the vehicle, taking their time. I said to the officer, 'Can you hurry up, mate? I've got a counselling session to go to.'

The police officer roared with laughter, so I told him about it: 'Seriously, mate, I was in a bad way, I got into drugs and violence and crime, but I called out to God and I'm turning my life around, and this counsellor is helping me do it. And if I'm not there by 4 p.m., he won't stay later at the end, so I don't want to be late.'

This copper just went, 'Either you're lying or you're bonkers. But either way, off you go.'

That's how much I valued that relationship, because I knew I needed it. How many men have that privilege?

Ian

When you make a decision to come to faith, however it happens, it doesn't stop there. You've got to find out more. You want to live the life, you need to be ready to respond to people when they ask you about your faith. You can't do that if you read the Bible once a month and only go to church when your wife drags you there.

You have to investigate the gospel – the claims of the gospel, the claims for the existence of God. Get a Bible, open the Bible, read the Bible. Take responsibility for your beliefs. Read the gospels, find out what Jesus said. You've got to challenge yourself intellectually with the words of Jesus, not just wait for some feeling or miracle – you've got to examine the words of Jesus, and work out how you're going to respond.

Arthur

I was talking to another guy after an event at a church once. He came up to us with his wife, and she said, 'Please can you talk to my husband.'

Well, that was funny to start with – she said that right in front of him, and he's standing there like a lemon, looking sheepish and sort of rolling his eyes at how she's talking about him.

So I said, 'What's up?'

He said, 'Well, you were talking about this feeling you had when you became a Christian – well, I don't have that – it just doesn't mean anything to me.'

I said, 'Son, the feeling's not the main thing. If I'd only had a feeling thirty years ago, I wouldn't still be here now, telling people about Jesus. That was the start of God's work in my life, but you've got to find out about God for yourself, see what he wants in your life. Don't worry about the feeling.'

Ian

When I was competing, I thought about my diet and I had an exercise programme. There was structure and discipline. I had guys I worked out with. I would look at what kind of training other people were doing, get advice, read about other bodybuilders. Otherwise, how could I progress?

It's the same with our faith. We have to investigate and learn. We need to be discipled. And we need good habits. That's why I wrote *Christ the Bodybuilder* – it explains the basics of the Christian faith, and then teaches men how to have good spiritual habits in life – reading the Bible, praying, belonging to a church.

We also need to be spending time with other guys who are committed to following Christ. This has been so key to Tough Talk over the years – being together, praying together, discussing the Bible together, challenging each other about our lives. There's no way we could have kept doing God's work without that fellowship and that accountability. All men need that.

Joe and I did a big men's conference, around 2015 or so. We spoke to probably over a thousand men. They actually gave us a standing ovation, which was a bit embarrassing.

On this occasion, Joe talked quite a lot about pornography. He had some struggles with pornography as a young man – both before Christianity but also when he was a Christian. He talked about how that damages your witness, damages your marriage, damages your life and the way you see other people. They'd asked us to do some prayer and ministry time, so at the end, I said, 'If you're particularly interested in having prayer to do with pornography, Joe will pray for you, and any other issues, come to this side, and I'll pray for you.'

Well, loads of men came up for prayer, but the majority of them joined Joe's queue. So, I prayed for the guys who had come forward to my side of the auditorium, and then I ended up helping Joe by praying for some of the men on his side too.

When I was growing up, pornography was for dirty old men. Now, it's so different. It's glamorised, seen as normal, and it's so easy to access. But it's not good. It's damaging in every way. It damages your walk with God and your friendships. It's damaging to your wife, it's damaging to someone who might become your wife.

Men are very susceptible to visual impulses. Most of the guys we prayed for were from a church background and to see so many of them struggling with this addiction was pretty sad.

At the same time, isn't that brilliant, that men will stand up and go, 'Yeah that's me,' and come and get help with sorting it out? There's power in confessing our sins to each other. You're more likely to do that at a men's conference, than when you're in your home church. The Bible says:

> If we say that we have fellowship with Him, and walk in darkness, we lie and do not practice the truth. But if we walk in the light as He is in the light, we have fellowship with one another, and the blood of Jesus Christ His Son cleanses us from all sin.
>
> *1 John 1:6–7, NKJV*

Well, if you're walking in pornography, you're not walking in the light. You're not going to be fruitful in the things of God. So let's deal with that.

However, once they've confessed their sin, and we've prayed for them, I also want to say to these guys, 'Get yourself out of this.'

Get out of this issue, and start preaching the gospel and get involved with the good things of God. If you're accessing pornography on your computer, put your computer away, or only use it in the kitchen where you can be seen, or stop staying late at the office. Whatever it is. The Bible says, 'Resist the devil and he will flee from you' (Jas 4:7, NKJV) and it also says, 'Seek first the kingdom of God and His righteousness' (Matt. 6:33, NKJV).

So don't just try and stop doing the harmful stuff – replace it with good stuff. And hang out with guys who will support you in that.

When you start to live and do the things of God, the temptations and evil that held you down often fall away. When you start being 'doers of the word' (Jas 1:22, NKJV), active in the word, then the things that were binding you, the things you were in thrall to, they get left behind.

If we spend hours just trying to work on the issues of pornography, it's like the dog returning to his vomit.[1] If you get up in the morning and think, 'This is the day the Lord has made, we're going to get out and do something useful for the kingdom,' then you have a mind and a purpose, and after a while, you will suddenly realise those chains have broken.

If I were a church pastor, I'd much rather take a few guys on a mission than spend hours with them counselling and talking through issues and problems. Get them out to another part of the country – or another country all together.

They don't have to be preaching. Get them to give out the shoes in an orphanage, or dig the well, or give out food. Whatever. Because then you're working together, and fellow-shipping together – you're a group of God-following men who are eating, fasting, praying, waking up together, chatting and doing the works of God.

That's what you see in the book of Acts – you see Peter, Paul, Silas and their friends bowling around, praying for people, eating together, fellowshipping together, preaching the gospel.

So, as the Bible says, let's 'cast off the works of darkness', and 'put on the armor of light' (Rom. 13:12, NKJV), and let's 'fight the good fight of faith' (1 Tim. 6:12, NKJV), taking up 'the sword of the Spirit, which is the word of God' (Eph. 6:17, NKJV). Let's get out there and do it.

> We must hold on to the hope we have, never hesitating to tell people about it. We can trust God to do what he promised.
> We should think about each other to see how we can encourage each other to show love and do good works. We must not quit meeting together, as some are doing. No, we need to keep on encouraging each other. This becomes more and more important as you see the Day getting closer.
>
> *Heb. 10:23–25, ERV*

Chapter Twelve

Amazing Grace

> Where sin abounded, grace abounded much more, so
> that as sin reigned in death, even so grace might reign
> through righteousness to eternal life through Jesus
> Christ our Lord.
>
> *Rom. 5:20–21, NKJV*

Arthur

Ian and I went out to South Africa together in 2013. Ian had
a black Freelander at the time, so he was driving to the airport.
I had moved to Cornwall by then, so I'd caught a train up to
Paddington, then got the Heathrow Express. When I arrived,
I went up to the check-in area. No Ian.

I waited for a bit, then a bloke from the airline came up to
me and said, 'Are you wanting to check in, sir?'

'No, it's alright,' I said. 'I'm waiting for my pal. He's on his
way. We're checking in together.'

'OK,' said the guy, but he looked a bit doubtful.

Then Ian phoned me and said, 'Arf! I've broken down on
the motorway!'

Ian

I'd left myself enough time – I thought – but I wasn't expecting to break down! It was a decent car, and not old, there was no reason for it to conk out, but it did. Also, it was raining.

The RAC guy had arrived, and I was standing on the hard shoulder getting absolutely soaked. I rang Arf and I had to tell him I didn't know if I'd make it. As I stood there getting wetter and wetter, I felt like the devil was trying to stop me getting to South Africa – and might be succeeding.

Then a car pulled up. A man jumped out and said, 'Here, mate, have an umbrella!' He handed me his umbrella, jumped back in his car, and drove off again.

You might think that's not much, but it was just enough to get my faith rising. I kind of thought, 'Well, the Lord cares about how wet I get, maybe he can sort out the trip as well.' And sure enough, they put my Freelander on the back of the truck and they started driving me to the airport.

Arthur

Meanwhile, the guy from the airline comes up to me again, and says, 'Mr White, you've really got to get on board. You can't wait any longer for your friend.'

I sighed. I didn't really fancy going on my own, but I didn't have much choice. I started walking towards departures with the airline representative. But as I turned to take one last look out of the airport doors, I saw an RAC vehicle pulling up, with Ian's car on the back! I beamed and shouted to the airport guy, 'Look! There's my mate! He's here!'

Ian

So, the first thing I saw as we arrived at the airport was Arthur's smiling face! The RAC dropped me off right outside the terminal. I jumped out of the truck, grabbed my bag, and raced over to Arf. We checked in, got ourselves through security and pretty much ran all the way to the plane.

It was only when we got on the flight that we realised neither of us had any idea where the RAC had taken my Freelander!

Arthur

I'd been out to South Africa once before, with a local church, St Mary's in Loughton. One of the members had a property in South Africa, and lived there half the time. He arranged for us to go out to do some evangelistic meetings, and he also organised for us to visit Pollsmoor Prison.

So, I didn't have Ian with me that time, just a small team from the church, including the vicar, and my wife, Jacqui.

Pollsmoor is the most notorious prison in South Africa. It was largely run by gangs, and it was also where they put Nelson Mandela after he came off Robben Island. They don't have cells as such in Pollsmoor, they have dormitories with thirty or forty men in them.

I remember the guards didn't come in with us. They opened the gate to the dorm, let us go in, then locked it behind us. It was as though they were saying, 'You wanted to go in – on your heads be it.' So, me and this nice vicar bloke got put into this cell with forty violent prisoners. And neither of us were too happy about it.

I started getting on with the job at hand. I was talking to the lads in there, telling them who we were, giving my testimony, saying, 'If Jesus came tomorrow, where would you stand?' and all that sort of thing. It did have a horrific smell in there, but I put that down to the fact that there were a couple of open toilets in the dorm, and no windows.

Anyway, I was talking away, and I sort of looked down to the floor, and there were a few charred lumps, like the remains of a campfire, so I said to the blokes, with a sort of chuckle, 'That your central heating, then, is it?'

One of the guys in the dorm – probably the one in charge – said, 'No. That's the remains of . . . ' and he said a man's name.

It all sort of went quiet. I just said, 'Oh,' and the vicar went as white as a sheet, and looked like he would be sick.

In South African prisons, there's something called the Numbers Gang. It's an immensely violent, immensely powerful network, and very rigid in structure, rules and organisation. There are three main gang groups, known by their numbers – 26, 27 and 28.

This fellow had done something to upset the gang. He had tried to get at the wrong person, or he'd broken a rule of some kind. So, what they did was, they wrapped him up in his mattress, and they set fire to him. So, we were looking at the remains of this body, burnt to a cinder with just ashen lumps on the floor, in the middle of the dormitory.

You could see why the guards weren't coming in.

I did another meeting in a different part of the prison another day, and this time I was on my own – it wasn't really planned. The guards were taking me past this section of the prison that had single cells, opening onto a sort of yard. It was open-air – no roof. It had double gates going into it, like an enclosure at a zoo, and the guards told me, as we were going past, that these were the most serious offenders in the prison.

So I said, 'Well, let me go in.'

Lifting the Darkness

They did the same thing as before. They pushed me through this gate and just left me. And I remember thinking, 'Why did I open my mouth?' And then I thought, 'Where's my mate, Ian?'

I was standing in the middle of this yard, with twenty or thirty blokes, staring at this strange man who just turned up out of the blue. I was trying to think quickly on my feet, but I'm not that quick at thinking, so I whistled! I whistled them over, and called, 'Come 'ere!' And they all sort of looked. I whistled again, and said, 'Come on! I want to tell you something.' And off I went . . .

'My name's Arthur White, and I'm a world champion powerlifter,' (I was still pretty big then) 'and I want to tell you this – that I was a drug addict. I was addicted to steroids and cocaine for ten years. But Jesus Christ came into my life.'

As soon as I mentioned Jesus, something changed in the atmosphere. There was a heightened awareness. Out in South Africa, they know there is a spiritual aspect to life. They know evil in a way that most people here in the West have been very, very shielded from. The name of Jesus is powerful, and cannot be ignored.

In our world, because things are generally comfortable, we get to ignore the spiritual reality. In their world, no way. There is violence happening all the time. It's all about who's got the power, and you're on one side or the other.

I gave my testimony, and I prayed. They all listened, but there was no warmth there, no tangible response, just a sort of alertness and tension. And then I remember turning around, thinking, 'I'm done, but where's the guard?'

There was this awful moment when I thought, 'I've told them all this stuff, and I'm still alone with them, and this could be indefinite.' They could easily have turned on me, torn me to pieces.

The guard did turn up and let me out again. So that was good. But it was one of the few times – I have to admit this – when I'd opened my mouth as a Christian, and thought, 'I wish I hadn't.' It really frightened me, and I remember thinking vividly, 'I wish Ian was here.'

Ian

After that visit, Arthur and I went out to South Africa a couple of times together, and basically, we did the prisons. We did a couple of schools, as well, but the prisons were the main work. We did Pollsmoor again, and also Drakenstein – which was more out in the bush, and was lower security.

We did a smaller, country prison as well – I remember staying out one night in a village hotel somewhere, near a farm. We sat on the balcony out front, and they brought us some steak, which turned out to be wildebeest! It was very nice.

I've never been anywhere quite like Pollsmoor. It was a large and very intimidating prison, full of strange contrasts. For example, you know they are violent criminals, but they're not fed very well – sometimes just some gruel in the morning – so they're skinny fellas. You're looking at these hardcore gangsters, tattooed everywhere, very hard faces, and they wouldn't hesitate to do whatever they wanted, and yet individually, they looked like you could bowl them over.

In one of the dormitories, a young fella sang to us. When we went in, they said, 'Oh, do you mind if so-and so-sings?'

We said, 'Sure,' and he sang. It was incredible. He sang some beautiful Motown songs. He had the most amazing voice. They told us, once a week the whole cell block raped him. He was their sex toy.

Some of them, quite a few, have no teeth. Other gang members have pulled their teeth out, so they can perform oral sex better. They're horrifically open about it. It's part of the set-up. And the guards let all this stuff go on, because it keeps the prisoners under control to some degree. They don't have a lot of choice. They let them police the place their own way. So, there's a lot of violence in there. Sex, money, drugs, violence, power.

We prayed between all our visits. I just remember praying, and thinking, 'I'm relying on you, Holy Spirit.' You can't go in with a half measure. Either you're sharing your faith or you're not. You've got to be honest and upfront with it. And incredibly, in this place of absolute filth and darkness, there's an understanding of the gospel.

We were downstairs at one point, and they were ushering all the guys up into a hall. I didn't know what was going on, but suddenly they all started singing 'Amazing Grace!'[1] And they could sing. What a sound! It was incredible – this beautiful hymn of repentance and praise resonating through the prison. I remember thinking, the gospel is here, already, before us. The light is somehow shining in this very, very dark place.

The particular story that has always stood out for me, in Pollsmoor, happened one afternoon. We'd been with the young offenders that morning, and we spent the afternoon in one of the adult dorms. There we were, locked in with some very dangerous characters, and we were sharing, and preaching the gospel, and there was a guy in the front, who kept interrupting to ask questions. One of the questions was, he asked me how I got out of the gang.

I realised that in my testimony I'd talked about being part of a gang before I was a Christian, and then afterwards I wasn't in that gang any more. I'd used the word 'gang' because I'd thought it would help them relate, but I quickly realised, his gang was different to mine. I had to explain to him, it wasn't a gang like in South Africa.

The guys I was working doors with, most of them had come together out of organised football hooliganism, back in the eighties and nineties. It was more like a firm – that's what we would have called it back then. It was an association of guys; you were on the same side and you watched each other's backs. We were violent men, on the whole, but it wasn't a gang with initiation ceremonies, secret languages, or bloodthirsty rites of passages.

I had to explain that it was a different type of scenario, and I kind of felt bad, because this guy was in the Numbers Gang. But this guy kept listening, and asking questions, and then a bit later on in the meeting, he said this to me,

'I've listened to you guys. I believe in Jesus. I believe that he died, and he rose again.' Then he went on, 'I want to be a Christian, but if I become a Christian today, I won't be alive in the morning. So, what should I do?'

The question hung in the air, and I wished he hadn't asked it.

He said to us, 'If I become a Christian, they will take my life during the night.'

What are you going to say to that?

'That's what will happen,' he continued. And then he added, 'I know, because I've carried this sentence out myself.'

I was stumped, because I was thinking, 'I've come here to preach the gospel, there's no other message that's relevant in this situation. There's nothing else – no other hope – I can give this guy. But if the price of this hope is quite literally his life, well, who am I to tell him which way to choose? Do I want to be the one responsible for him losing his life tonight?'

I was prevaricating a bit, rubbing my chin as if I was thinking about the question, when Arthur, standing next to me, said, 'Can I answer that?'

'Yeah, please do, Arf, all yours.' I doubtless sounded a bit relieved.

Arthur looked at this young man, and he said, 'Son, it's like this . . . Through the abuse of steroids and cocaine, I've got metal shoulders, metal hips and metal knees. I've had five operations on my heart. I've been told by the doctor that I could have a heart attack or a stroke at any time. I know that I could die at any moment.' Then he said,

'Listen, son. I'm in a win-win situation. Because if I live, I'm living with Jesus. And if I die, I'm going to be with Jesus. We all live inside a body. Our bodies are going to die one day, but the real person, inside, will at some point be standing before our Maker, giving an account of his life. Now is the moment. Get right with God.'

After that, we led the guys in prayer. A number of them responded that day. They all bowed their heads, and I remember that fellow with tears in his eyes, as we prayed for them to receive Jesus Christ. It was one of those very precious moments. God is always at work, but sometimes you find yourself in a very particular 'God' place. You know you're operating in a moment that somehow carries more weight than most, almost as though it's a slice across time.

I've told that story many times over the years, and people will often say to me, 'Did he die? Did he survive?' And the answer is, we don't know. But the point is not whether he lived or died. The point is, that God is the God of the living, not the dead.[2] So if he did lose his life that night – and I prayed he didn't – I will still see him again.

Christians over here in the West, I think, don't really believe in the same way that this message is about life and death. We half-believe it, but not sincerely to the point where we're going to become radical disciples, give our lives for the cause of the gospel, and stake everything on eternity.

I mean, it's good to help people be clothed, and fed, and homed – all of that is good, godly stuff. But if you're measuring success that way, then it's a false economy, isn't it? Because what if you feed and clothe someone all their life, but they still don't turn to Christ? So, the answer Arthur gave is the truth, and it's a truth that we should all be operating in, as far as I'm concerned. We are often very removed from death in our society. The guys we met over in South Africa don't have that luxury – but it means they grasp the gospel better than a lot of us Westerners.

Arthur

Charles Spurgeon said, 'Death is no punishment to the believer. It is the gate of endless joy.'[3] And that's the truth.

The preacher Paul Washer says something like this: Jesus Christ only promises you two things: an eternal salvation to hope in; and a cross to die on.[4] Now, that is not a sentiment you will often hear. More often, you'll hear a message that makes out like Jesus promised you a nice house, or a great marriage, or good grades for your kids, or a handy parking space just outside the Co-op. But actually, Jesus says, 'In this world you will have trouble' (John 16:33, NIV) and he says, 'Take up your cross and follow me',[5] and he says, 'I am with you always, to the very end of the age' (Matt. 28:20, NIV).

There was one young fella in another prison – I think he'd been in for eight years, maybe longer – and he was a proper little fighter. You could see he'd been bashed up a few times. He'd got caught stealing so they put him in prison. But his case had never come to court, because to go to court, you have to pay – you or someone in your family, or a friend – and this lad, he had no family, or they couldn't find his family, and he had nothing, so he was just banged up in prison. For years. Without a trial. He was a bit aggressive and he could bite. I remember he looked like a little boxer. He was always in trouble, and course all they did was just bash him up and keep him locked up.

These things break your heart, really. I would find myself scared and heartbroken at the same time, as I went around the prisons there. The Lord has shown us a great variety of things around the world, and personally I find it hard to handle sometimes. I say to the Lord, 'Why do we see so much? Why do you show us so much evil?'

On the last evening of that trip, we were told we were doing an outreach in a school out in the bush. But we went, and there was nobody there. The school had packed up and closed, and the whole place was deserted. We turned to the guys who were meant to be organising this event, and we said, 'There's no one here!' But they said, 'Don't worry. It's going to be packed in about ten minutes.' I was in disbelief. I couldn't believe it, because it didn't look like there was anything or anyone for miles around. But the guys started setting up. They put up a PA, and they had cool boxes full of ice lollies the church had donated for the kids.

We set up our weights, and the sun was going down and I was thinking, 'Well, this is beautiful – this bush backdrop, the lowering light, the orange and purple sky.' It was just like the movies. Except there was no audience. Then suddenly, in the dusky light, kids started to appear. I don't know where they came from, it just sort of happened. Hundreds of little fellas, just skipping in, walking in from every direction, it was like magic. In they came and sat down on the ground in front of us.

We did some weights, and we shared our stories, Ian preached the gospel and there were all these lovely faces smiling up at us – such beautiful little souls!

Ian

When we got to praying the prayer of salvation, all their little heads bowed. I quite often say the prayer line by line, and invite people to repeat it after me, and they all did. There was this crowd of beautiful little children praying the prayer of life, and to be honest, it was very emotional.

What a contrast, seeing something of the beauty of humanity and the precious innocence of those children, after what we'd seen earlier that day. It was an incredible blessing for us – a reminder of God's love, and that he has, actually, made us all beautiful.

In that prison, we saw what happens when evil ruins God's creation. Then out in the bush, God reminded us of the absolute beauty of humanity how he created and intended it.

> Where sin increased, there was even more of God's grace. Sin once used death to rule us. But God gave us more of his grace so that grace could rule by making us right with him. And this brings us eternal life through Jesus Christ our Lord.
>
> *Rom. 5:20–21, ESV*

Chapter Thirteen

The Gospel on the Roof

Where can I go from Your Spirit?
Or where can I flee from Your presence?
If I ascend into heaven, You are there;
If I make my bed in hell, behold, You are there.

Ps.139:7–8, NKJV

Ian

I have never seen traffic like I saw in the Philippines – not even in India. Absolute gridlock, from start to finish. Nobody moves on the roads, they just sit there honking their horns all day and all night. I never worked out what they were trying to achieve with that horn-honking. It's not like anybody hasn't noticed you're there. It's not like anyone can do anything about it!

We were picked up from the airport and driven to our accommodation. It took hours. And when we got to the accommodation, we discovered it was right next to the road. All you could hear was honking horns, morning till night. It was a beautiful country, but I didn't sleep a lot in the Philippines.

Arthur

We got to our digs, and they were horrid. I don't know what you would class it as, certainly not a hotel. There were cockroaches in the corners, great big lizards running across the ceiling. The toilet was just a hole in the floor. In the morning, they left breakfast outside the door. It was a plate of rice and scrambled egg, and they just left it on the floor outside – where things could crawl on it. It was disgusting. It was a beautiful country, but I didn't eat a lot in the Philippines.

Ian

We went to the Philippines in February 2015. My home church, City Gates in Ilford, supported a church and a school out there, and the pastor of that church had invited us. Like in South Africa, the main thing was to go into the local prison, but we did a bit of schools work too. We had a few people from the church there helping us out, including an English lady who lived there as a missionary and acted as our interpreter. From the UK it was Arthur, me and young Luke.

Luke was the son of our pastor, Steve, and he was about 25 years old. He was a really nice lad, very dedicated and willing. He'd helped set up the visit, as he was pretty handy with booking the accommodation and doing the logistics, and he came on the team as well, and into the prison with us.

Arthur

The prison was on the outskirts of Manila, in an area called Antipolo – Antipolo City Jail. Antipolo is about 20km outside

Manila, but it felt like about 200km, driving there! I remember seeing a Holiday Inn from the road, and thinking, 'I wish we were staying there.'

It was a large prison, and it was awful. Horrendous. Phenomenal. Just getting through the gates was bad enough. There were a lot of guards, all armed to the teeth with guns and looking very, very suspicious. I don't think many people went to visit the guys in prison. I suppose that's why we were there.

Ian

The prison smelt like death. I grew up around a veterinary surgery, so I know what dead things smell like. It was a stench. We did a couple of meetings in the morning, and a couple in the afternoon. In-between, they showed us round the prison.

I saw a whiteboard. In most prisons they have a board like that, for roll count and keeping track of the prisoners. I was looking at this whiteboard, which said 'fifty' in the first box, and then 'thirty-seven' in the next, and I was thinking, right, there's fifty men in the first wing, and thirty-seven in the next wing. But as we went down, I realised it wasn't wings, it was cells. There were fifty men in one cell, and in the cell next door, there were thirty-seven women.

The cell was like a cage. It had three walls, iron bars on the front, and only part of it had a roof. There were three beds on the wall. Three beds for fifty men. They had to sleep in rotation. There was a gully running down the middle of the cell, which was an open sewer. They were squashed so tightly together, they could hardly squat down. It was probably the most disgusting place I've ever seen.

Next door, the women's cell was much the same, except that there was a washing line strung across that one, because the women were trying to do their laundry. You couldn't imagine anyone even trying to keep clean in a place like that.

There was a young fella at the front of the men's cell. His faced was pressed against the bars, his face was full of fear, and his eyes were wide like saucers – massive wide eyes. He looked like he was about to die. I couldn't walk past him. He was so distressed my heart was moved for him. I remember saying through the interpreter, 'Can I pray for this lad?'

The interpreter said, 'You'll have to ask the mayor.'

I was so confused. I said, 'What do you mean? We haven't got time to go see the mayor to say a prayer for this fellow.'

Then a big guy right at the back of the cell jumped down self-importantly from the bed he'd been sitting on. He had a stick and various bits of paraphernalia. He started wading through the other inmates, scuffing people out of the way, hitting them with his stick. This geezer was the mayor of the cell! It was a sandwich-packed cell of hellish humanity, and he was in charge of it.

We were watching him push and hit his way through to the front of the cell, and I was half-wishing I'd never started this thing. Then we saw that he had got a dog with him! The mayor was strong. The other guys looked like they hadn't eaten for weeks, but the mayor was fat. He had this dog, a skinny little mutt, who came forward with him, and if I remember rightly, the dog came forward with him, and then just kept walking, straight through the bars of the cell, he was that skinny. The dog walked out, walked around us, then walked back in again to the mayor.

So, I'm having a word with this mayor, through the interpreter, saying, 'Can I pray for this guy?' and the mayor is humming and hawing, sort of making a play of weighing up my request – and finally he gives me permission to pray for the young guy.

I stood by the bars and prayed for this young man. He looked so petrified. I prayed with him, talked to him, and I'd like to say he got some comfort from the prayer, but I don't know. To tell the truth, I was in shock at the whole situation. Even compared to South Africa, the conditions were appalling. We were really just trying to get our heads round the place. And this young man with his enormous, terrified eyes, I couldn't ignore him.

Arthur

We weren't sure where we were going to do our presentations, but they said, 'We'll do it on the roof.'

So off we went up towards the roof. It was the only place they could gather the prisoners together in a group. There was no hall, no exercise yard, no dining area, nothing, just a couple of storeys of cells, and a flat roof on top. We hadn't brought our own weights with us, but the church had managed to get a little bit of rough-and-ready equipment, and the prison presented us with a barbell, which was their gym. It was a bar with a lump of concrete stuck on either end. It looked ridiculous – not even very heavy! But we said 'thank you', and up we went.

Well, even getting up onto the roof was interesting. They had this very rickety bamboo ladder, like a bit of bamboo scaffolding running up the outside of the building, and all the prisoners, and all the guards, and us and the equipment all had to get up there via this little ladder made of bamboo, on the exterior of the building. I remember thinking, 'I don't know if I'm going to make it.'

Ian

I went up behind Arthur, and he's a big bloke, and at the time was in his sixties already. I remember thinking, 'I hope he's going to make it, because if he falls, I'm done for.' Then on the way back down, stupidly, I went before Arf. And I remember again, looking up and seeing his big old body and his big old legs, and his metal knees, and thinking, 'If he falls, I'm still done for! Why didn't I let him go down first?'

Arthur

So, there we are, up on a roof in the Philippines, with fifty criminals who live crammed into one cell, a load of guards with guns, us, our interpreter and young Luke.

The charity which this church ran had funded some food and fizzy drinks, so they all got something to eat and drink on the roof. Even just that was a big deal – getting out of that awful cell for an hour or so, getting something to eat – possibly for the first time in ages, to judge by how they looked. I should think it might have been the only time some of them had been out of their cell since being put in prison.

There was a small parapet wall around the roof, but otherwise it was completely open. You could see the canopy of the jungle just beyond. So at least there was some air. The guards were initially pretty twitchy, worried that the prisoners would try to jump off the roof to escape, even though it was a good two storeys high, but they settled down after a bit.

Ian

What are you going to preach, standing on that prison roof with these men and their wretched existence? You can't preach, 'Life is going to get good for you,' or the hope of parole, or turning away from crime – I mean, nothing of that makes sense. You've got to preach a hardcore gospel – there is a God, he knows you, you're going to face him one day. It's the gospel of life and death, and you could tell that some of the men there weren't going to make it. They weren't going to get out of that place alive, and it might not take long.

So, you want to say to these men that there is more than this grotty, material reality. You want to say, 'You are a human being with a soul. You are a spiritual being, and God is a spiritual being, and that part of you will survive, will persist. There is hope. Trust in Jesus Christ as Lord and Saviour.'

We spoke a clear message, and we had a good time there in the way of ministry. God encountered people. We presented challenges, and many of those men responded. I mean, it's an absolute hellhole, so of course everyone is putting their hand up, saying, 'I want a bit of Jesus,' no doubt about it. But God knows what's going on, on the inside, and I felt like it was very genuine. To me, it definitely felt like it ignited something in those guys – a new flame of faith. The guards responded too, in fact. Some of them were quite touched.

Arthur

It was a great privilege to be able to share with these guys that there is hope. We gave our testimonies, but even with whatever hell we've been through, we couldn't possibly look those men in the eye and say, 'I know how you feel.' I love the testimonies, but actually, to hear Ian preach the gospel on that roof, to say, 'There is hope for your souls' – that was a great privilege.

Ian

In Western Europe, we look to the prison system for the possibility of reform, as well as punishment. The deprivation of liberty is punishment in itself. There are programmes to help you not reoffend. I'm not saying it's perfect, but the basic outlook is rehabilitation and hope.

In most of the world, it's not like that – you're in prison because you committed a crime, and you're there being punished. Full stop. If you die in there, that's your lookout. If you get sexually assaulted in there, that's your problem. Life and death are cheap.

Arthur

It was total misery in there. It's hard to explain – and even at the time, it was hard to grasp. You've gone from your normal life, almost like in through the gates of hell. Even now, looking back on it, I'm wondering what happened to that little lad that Ian prayed for. It was just shocking. Even just going to the toilet – a channel in the middle of the cell – it's disgusting. I mean, I've worked in sewers – I've done work building drains and sewers – I know how it smells. But I didn't have to lie in them, day and night.

We got rid of that sort of system in the British prisons 300 or 400 years ago. Even in the cold, hard days of slopping out in the sixties, it was a lot better. You'd have to go back almost to the sixteenth century to see that sort of filth and darkness.

The interesting thing was, for the guards, it clearly felt normal. They weren't shocked by it. Maybe they'd become hardened to it. I guess they haven't seen any different. From our perspective, it was a hellhole, and it seemed odd that they weren't embarrassed to show it to someone from outside, but to them, this is how things are.

The guards themselves were well-presented. They had a nice uniform, were smiling and friendly. It's a beautiful country – there's sunshine, there are lovely people outside, great hospitality, great warmth. Yet among all that, there's this level of darkness that you wouldn't even see in the UK. It's beyond our comprehension, really. We've been to prisons in a lot of places, but that was one of the most shocking things we've ever seen. I don't think I've ever seen so much fear in men as I saw there.

Ian

In Britain, although we're not a Christian country any more, we have a long history of Christianity informing the state and the state institutions, including prisons. So, Christianity brought the idea of reform, and also the sense that everyone has value. People in our country don't realise it – they take our values for granted – but Christianity is what everything is built on. That's why we have chaplains in all the prisons. It goes back to the times of the Wesley brothers, George Whitefield and those great reformers.

The Philippines is quite a Christian country compared to England now. It is around 86 per cent Catholic. There are a lot of Christians, and a strong sense of morality, but they don't have that centuries-old Christian, or Judeo-Christian, world-view that our nation's foundations are built on.

People will ask me if my faith gets rocked seeing things like that prison, but to be honest, it rocks my faith in humanity, rather than in God. The inhumanity of man to his fellow man is not a pleasant thing to witness. All we can do is just keep focused on Jesus.

We can't allow things around us to affect our faith. Whether it's answered prayer, unanswered prayer, hellish conditions in prison, people surviving on gruel with maggots floating around in it, people being abused, famine around the world, loved ones dying. It's not relevant to look at that and then let that rot my faith in God.

I've looked at the world already, and it's got no attraction for me. So, it doesn't surprise me when I see grim stuff in the world. It may shock me, but it doesn't surprise me. I've seen evil, and I've seen good. I've looked at what the world has to offer, and it's pointless and meaningless. I think, there has to be a Creator, that's all that makes sense for me. I've experienced the goodness of God, and I know there's a battle on between good and evil.

The experience I had the night of my conversion was supernatural, so I believe there's a supernatural God. And from that experience, I've investigated the truth of Jesus Christ and his Word. I've become convinced that Jesus Christ crucified is the only message that makes sense of our predicament, so that message has to get preached. There's more than the here and now.

I'm thankful that we had a few moments telling those guys that there is love and hope. There aren't many evangelists going into prisons like that. It was a privilege. It was an unpleasant, upsetting, dirty, smelly, disgusting privilege to be there.

The women also came up for a presentation on the roof, and they responded to God too. There was a sense of openness. I think seeds of faith were sown. But as the women were starting to leave, one of the guards came to young Luke, and asked him if he wanted to choose one of them to spend an hour with. Luke came over and told me what had just happened. He was shocked, and astonished, and so was I, really. I said, 'What did you do?'

'I politely declined.'

'Good lad.'

How do you get your head round that? You've gone in there as a group of Christians, preaching Jesus, and they offer to pimp out one of the women prisoners for you. In that stinking hole of a place! What are they thinking? You can't get your head around it. To say that to a young Christian minister. I guess the guard thought he might get a couple of quid out of it. I don't know. I don't want to think about it.

I don't know if I can even explain just how dark, how oppressive that place was – how those people were on the very edge of their existence, their humanity. It was a lot to deal with – and I've seen a lot of grim stuff in my life. In that beautiful country, with those warm and welcoming people, suddenly you go through a set of prison gates and it's like you've stepped into a version of hell.

But God was present, in that place, so who are we to say we won't go there?

Your Spirit is everywhere I go. I cannot escape your presence. If I go up to heaven, you will be there. If I go down to the place of death, you will be there.

Ps. 139:7–8, ERV

Chapter Fourteen

The Wrong Part of Town

The LORD is my light and my salvation; whom shall I fear?
The LORD is the strength of my life; of whom shall
I be afraid?

Ps. 27:1, NKJV

Ian

It was later in 2015 that we went to Lebanon. There was a guy called Jean-Louis who was from Beirut. He came to England as a refugee, with a drug addiction and alcohol problem. He went through the Teen Challenge drug rehab programme for eighteen months, got clean and became a Christian. I first met him when I was speaking there, years ago, then he went full circle and started working for Teen Challenge, then LCM, and then he joined City Gates Church in Ilford.

He asked me if I would come to Beirut and share the gospel with an Elim church out there and he also asked Luke, who we went to the Philippines with. Luke and Jean-Louis then organised the visit together, booking the flights and making the arrangements. Luke was dating my daughter by this time, so I was also his prospective father-in-law.

I asked Arthur if he fancied coming, but I didn't put any pressure on. I was aware, no matter what the political climate, that Beirut is a hotbed – right in the heart of the Middle East, bordering Israel and Syria, not far from Jordan, Palestine, the West Bank. We were advised not to let anyone know where we were going, or to mention on social media where we would be staying. The civil war in Syria was kicking off, with the Russians' involvement. ISIS was just over the border. Where we were going was quite close to a Hezbollah part of town. Basically, there was a possibility that a Westerner could get kidnapped – that was the thought process – so I wasn't going to force anything.

However, Arthur said yes, and we arrived in Beirut, which was quite an eye-opener in itself. This place used to be the jewel of the Mediterranean, and later on in the trip, we went up to see the cedars on Mount Lebanon, which are mentioned many times in the Bible and are just beautiful. But your first impression is it looks like a dump.

It was dark. A lot of the buildings were still in ruins. The houses were small and close together, with electricity cables sagging from every corner. At the time, I remember, the minister in charge of refuse disposal had embezzled all the money, so there were no refuse collections. The whole city was overflowing with bags of rubbish. It was madness.

It looked like there had just been a war. The civil war, which absolutely ravaged the place, had ended twenty-five years earlier, but the most recent war was only nine years before, and there were regular border clashes and uprisings.

We were working with this Elim church, and we slept in their basement. The pastor there was a great guy. He was working with Muslim refugees coming over from Syria. We were there for the best part of a week. The plan was to do some outreach alongside the church, and one of the highlights was going to be speaking at a gym in downtown Beirut.

Arthur

The first night, I stepped out of the church into the streets, and I could hear people praising God in the distance. The part of town we were in had a lot of Coptic Christians, and there was another church nearby. There was an atmosphere of darkness, yet there was a strong Christian presence.

When we were going round the streets, we could identify the different communities. In one street, you'd have a cross hanging, and that was the Christian quarter, so you'd walk around there quite happily. Then you'd turn a corner, and the next street had an Islamic symbol or sign and you knew that was a different neighbourhood, so you didn't walk down that one.

There was great religious division. The civil war there, between Christian and Muslim political factions, lasted fifteen years and ended in 1990. It was very much in people's memories. Nearly every household had a gun. You felt you were in a very volatile situation.

Syria was very close – it was about fifty miles from Beirut to the border. Our hosts took us up a mountain to a shrine at one point – Our Lady of Lebanon, it was called. There was a large monument, with big cedar trees, and from the viewpoint, they pointed out the sights: 'There's Syria over that way, and that's the West Bank. If you drove down that road there, you'd be at the Israeli border.'

We had lunch at a restaurant, on the coast. They brought us a magnificent platter of fresh fruit. As we ate it, along up the coast, I saw a plume of smoke. I said to the waiter, 'What's that?'

He shrugged and said, 'Oh, it's another bomb gone off in Syria.'

So, you have this awful contrast – you're eating this delicious platter of fresh fruit, all juicy and sweet, looking out over the sparkling Mediterranean Sea, yet you're sitting a few miles away from where a bomb's gone off, and there's rubbish in all the streets because the government's not really functioning properly, and each street is a different faction to the next.

It just felt volatile the whole time we were there. Volatile was definitely the word for it.

Ian

We did one meeting with the church, with the Syrian refugees they were supporting. There were lots of girls wearing *hijabs*, and they were giving witness to how the Holy Spirit was changing their lives. It was incredible. They were still wearing the *hijab*, but since coming over from Syria, they had been welcomed and fed by the Christians in Lebanon, and they were really open to hearing about their faith. So, we were preaching the gospel, and people were responding.

We did a couple of church meetings. I don't think we lifted any weights, we just spoke and gave testimony at the churches. They were good meetings. We were really bringing the gospel message. The church members were kind of fascinated that we English people were there, and interested that we would be bothered to go over and support them while they were in the process of caring for these refugees.

There was a barbecue one night up on a roof. It was a large, wide, flat roof. These Christians were cooking food for everyone – the church, the neighbours, the refugees – it was a beautiful thing to see. But if you looked out across the roof-tops, the city was in a state of devastation. You could see what an awful place it was to live, yet in the midst of that, people were showing love and grace to each other.

Another of the things the church had lined up for us was a visit to a local gym. It was the three of us – me, Arthur and Luke. The point was to connect with the rough men who went to this gym, who were arming themselves for war.

The Christian areas were caught in the middle, geographically, between Hezbollah in Lebanon and ISIS in Syria. I think at that point they were more afraid of ISIS than Hezbollah. So, the people in the Christian areas of the city said openly, 'Let them come, we're going to slaughter them. We are preparing for battle.' That was their reality. They had been in civil war and a state of up-heaval for so long, they were prepared to fight and stand up for what they believed was right. These were men from the Christian communities. I guess you could call them nominal Christians – the average people on the streets in the Christian areas. They had decided they'd had enough of being destroyed. They were arming themselves and training themselves, getting ready.

So, this was a hardcore gym that we did the meeting in. A proper spit-and-sawdust place, packed with large lumps of men. We met the owner. His cousin was a man called Samir Bannout, who was a former Mr Lebanon and Mr Olympia. I'd seen Samir around a bit in the bodybuilding world, so we had some common ground there.

We didn't do a demonstration that night, we just went in to give testimony and share our faith. The gym owner went round to them all, stopping their training and waving them over to gather and listen to us. That was a bit awkward. These guys properly got the hump, because they weren't expecting us – we weren't advertised or anything; they were just there at the gym, and they wanted to get on with their training.

Arthur

I remember, they looked so aggrieved to be summoned over to hear us. Ian took me aside and said to me, 'You gotta tell them from the off, all your titles, and your records, and your weights.' So I did. I made a point of puffing up my chest a bit and listing my titles and achievements, which of course were impressive – and I knew what I had lifted would be more than they would have done. Then they were like, 'Wow, we've got a seminar here with a world champion powerlifter!' So on the back of that, having got a bit of respect, we gave testimony and preached the gospel.

Ian

We really gave our hardcore testimony to these blokes and preached the gospel, and from that initial scepticism, there was actually a tremendous response. People were asking God into their lives. They were praying with us, asking questions, everything. One guy said to me, 'A year ago, none of these men would have stood and listened to this message, but the way things are now, life and death are more real – people are more open.'

However, our success was really almost our downfall at that point, because we had had such a good response that the owner of the gym asked our host, Jean-Louis, if we would visit another gym over in another part of town, owned by the president of the Lebanese powerlifting association.

There were some discussions between the owner of the gym and Jean-Louis, about visiting this other gym. Luke and Arf and I didn't know what they were saying to each other, as they were speaking either Arabic or French, but eventually they said, 'It'll be safe, let's go!' So, we got in this car.

This was actually our last night staying in Lebanon. We had a few hours before we needed to get to the airport. We set off driving through the backstreets of Beirut, and then we went into an underpass, quite an extensive one, a tunnel, really.

As we emerged, it was like the world had transformed. All you could see were black, Islamic flags everywhere. The atmosphere took a turn as well. We may have come from a part of town that looked like a recent warzone, but this part looked like we might just get locked up and never come home. I felt a real darkness come over me.

We pulled up outside an incredible building, and inside there was the most enormous, state-of-the-art gymnasium. None of us had ever seen anything like it. There were huge lumps all over the place, looking at us like we were the takeaway meal someone had just delivered. We got taken into the gym, and they introduced us.

As we were getting out of the car, we'd been told, 'Don't say anything about being Christian, because that won't be healthy for us.' So, I was thinking, 'What's the point of us being here, then? What's the purpose?' I felt very much in other people's hands.

It turned out that the purpose was really a political friendship game for the owner of the gym we'd been at earlier. He wanted to show off to the president of the Lebanese powerlifting association that he had Arthur White in his car.

The owner of this second gym came straight out to meet and greet this world champion powerlifter, and from then on, it was all about Arthur. Luke and I were mere accessories.

The place, as it turned out, wasn't so much a gym as a terrorist training centre. Literally. They had a load of guns and a firing range as well as numerous workout stations. They said to me and Luke, 'Do you want to have a go on the firing range while Arthur gets shown around?'

'No, thanks, no, I'd rather not,' I said.

Apart from anything else, I didn't think it would be helpful to me if they realised I'm not that great with a gun.

Arthur

It was a phenomenal gym. I've never seen equipment like it. It was like something out of a James Bond film. Red and white leather, glass and chrome, air-conditioning, then the gun range and assault courses and stuff outside. It must have cost an absolute fortune to build. There were tons and tons of weights – I mean, loads and loads of them. It was by far the best-equipped gym I've ever seen.

The guy in charge was talking about lifters he'd seen when he was travelling abroad, and lots of names that I also knew, and we were comparing notes about powerlifting, so I was just enjoying talking to someone so knowledgeable about my sport. In the back of my mind, though, I could tell we weren't in the right place politically – or spiritually. We were in a very dangerous situation, no doubt about it. But I wasn't sure what I could do about that, except to keep admiring the gym and talking about lifting.

Ian

Arthur was definitely the centre of attention, in this futuristic sort of powerlifting palace, and it seemed to us that he was oblivious to our discomfort. The guy showing us round was high up in all sorts of areas – he was active and senior in Hezbollah, as far as we could tell. He proudly showed us some photos taken the day before, when he'd been out on the streets with his kids all dressed in army combats, and him holding a machine gun, shooting in the air.

Arthur

All the guys training at the gym had bandanas on their heads, like you see in a hostage video. And this really was very close, geographically, to where Terry Waite had been kidnapped, so we were right in the lions' den. Ian had heard Terry Waite give his testimony just a few weeks before; I remembered him telling me about it. So, I was thinking, 'This could be it, this could be us done,' and all I wanted to do was keep this fellow sweet and keep talking about lifting.

Ian

The whole gym visit, Luke kept saying to me, 'Doesn't Arthur realise what danger we're in? Can't you get him to hurry up?' But when we looked at Arf, he'd be transfixed by some state-of-the-art kit or other. He was all over it: 'Ooh, this is a such-and-such bar! And that one – is that a so-and-so? And what does this one do?' He was like a child in a sweetshop, all bright-eyed and thrilled with it all, like we'd walked into some powerlifting heaven.

Mind you, I think that was probably what kept us safe – the pure innocent enthusiasm of Arthur White in a perfect powerlifting gym!

Arthur

To be honest, I knew he wanted Arthur White the powerlifter, so that's what I gave him. I never normally vaunt my powerlifting achievements. If someone recognises me in the gym, I just shrug it off – I'm an old has-been. But this time, I really went for it.

Ian

I felt like we might as well have had 'Kidnap me!' written across our foreheads. I'm convinced if the guy in charge had said, 'We'll have these three fellas,' that would have been it – although to be honest, there would have been a chance that they would've taken me and Luke, and let Arthur go free!

I teased Luke a bit. I said, 'Look, I'm carrying Arthur White's bags. I'll be alright, but what about you?' That was naughty of me, but I couldn't resist winding him up a bit.

I don't know how long we were at that gym. It was probably an hour, but it felt like the longest hour of my life. I think Luke probably aged about five years in that hour! We were offered some hospitality and we were trying to politely decline without offending someone. All we could think of was getting out.

Apart from the gym owner, who was all over Arthur, you could see there was tension among the other guys. People weren't happy at our presence there. I honestly think we were close to getting kidnapped that night.

We did get out, thankfully. We said our goodbyes. I had to almost peel Luke off the floor. We got back in the car, and I kept thinking, any minute now a vehicle's going to pull over in front of us, and stop the jeep, a load of guys with guns will jump out, and we'll be in body bags before we know where we are. My heart was in my mouth.

When we got back through the underpass, and that first bit of tension released, I turned round in the car to Jean-Louis, and said, 'Jean-Louis, what the heck was that?'

Jean-Louis just crumbled. He brought his hands together, and said, 'Please forgive me, please forgive me, that was dangerous, I'm so sorry, we should never have been there; you guys' lives were in danger.'

He had connected the dots and realised we shouldn't have been there, but too late – he couldn't do anything about it. It was very naughty, really, of the first gym guy – he was just using us to improve his own standing in the eyes of this big number at the other gym. There was no godly reason for us to be there. Actually, I think it was a move of the devil. But God kept us safe.

Arthur

On the journey back in the jeep, I got a text on my phone. There we were, bumping through the dark streets, between the high, crowded buildings and the electricity cables strung out everywhere, and my phone beeped.

I was the only one who'd got my phone out – I think I'd used it in the gym – it was such a beautiful place, I'd taken a few photos. I looked, and there was a text, saying something like: 'Mr White. This is the Foreign Office here. Are you OK?' Apparently we had been in an area that British citizens were advised not to travel to.

Young Luke was doing buttons.

Ian

To be honest, I didn't properly relax until Arf and I were up in the aircraft on the way home that evening. There were half a dozen security checks just to get in the airport. We went through check-in and luggage search. Even as we walked up the stairs to get on the plane, I saw they were stopping people again. They had plain clothes security guards at the plane door, looking at everyone's passports, and I even saw them turn a couple of people away.

I didn't really breathe properly until we were in our seats and the plane had taken off.

The ironic thing was, Luke had done the planning for the trip, and decided to stay on a few days with Jean-Louis for some sightseeing. Arthur and I aren't bothered with sightseeing – we like our missions to be missions and our holidays to be holidays, so we'd booked on a plane straight home. But Luke had thought he'd just do a couple of extra days. It had seemed a good idea at the time, but I'm not sure he did much sightseeing in the end – I think he just probably stayed in his room until it was time to go to the airport, trying not to think about the fact that Arf and I were home and dry.

Even now, when I see Jean-Louis he still apologises to me for that visit. But you have to trust that God was with us, somehow, and even though it was a mistake at the time, he will use it in some way for his glory.

We were asked if we'd go out to Lebanon again, and the invitation is open. That first meeting we'd done in the original gym had had a great response. Seeing the church there, and their work with the refugees was good too. We spoke at a couple of other, smaller churches too, and that was purposeful and positive, so it was a fruitful time overall. But there was no purpose going to that second gym.

You have to weigh these things up. You don't need to put yourself in harm's way for its own sake. If there's a volatile situation and you don't need to be there, don't go there.

If you're somewhere the Lord wants you to be, that's different – it's a calling or purpose, and you go. If I felt a strong conviction that God was calling us to Beirut again, I wouldn't hesitate. But I'm not going to start pushing on a door for no reason.

Arthur

I think I would have to have literally an audible voice from the Lord to get me out there again.

Ian

In 2021, there was a huge warehouse explosion that devastated a whole area of Beirut, by the port. It was in the news. The church we had worked with got destroyed in that blast. But the pastor is still out there ministering.

That pastor was a lovely guy. To me, he was the kind of Christian that I wouldn't be surprised if he was martyred for the faith. Occasionally, you meet a real Christian, and he was really one of them. I remember thinking, he's the real deal, this fellow. He was Jesus all over.

> LORD, you are my Light and my Savior, so why should I be
> afraid of anyone?
> The LORD is where my life is safe, so I will be afraid
> of no one!
>
> *Ps. 27:1, ERV*

Chapter Fifteen

Squatting for Jesus

> Yea, though I walk through the valley of the shadow of
> death, I will fear no evil; For You are with me; Your rod
> and Your staff, they comfort me.
>
> *Ps. 23:4–5, NKJV*

Arthur

Around 2016, we were invited to Romania, to visit the prisons
there. We were hosted by a church, who also provided some
interpreters to work with us.

It was Europe, but it was about as different to home as
South Africa had been, and also full of contrasts. One time,
we went up in the hills and saw an English fellow living there
in a sort of commune. They were all just living off the land,
without possessions, sharing what they made and grew.

There was a lot of poverty and deprivation, but Joe, Ian and
I stayed in a hotel! It was a fancy place with a swimming pool
and everything, but it was not at all expensive. There was an
extreme difference between how we were living, and how they
were living.

One of our days there, we went into a Romany settlement – and it really was a settlement – sheds and tarpaulin houses. We did an outreach, and there were people sitting there on the mud tracks between the houses listening to us. It wasn't nice. It stank. There were little kids without clothes on and women with no shoes. It felt pretty incongruous, rolling out our lifting gear.

We went into a few different prisons, and everywhere we went, we were met with initial hostility. I mean, we're often not greeted with open arms, but in a lot of places there is some curiosity – or even a sense that at least something different is happening other than the same old prison routine. But in Romania, there was a lot of hostility.

We had two interpreters – a young woman and a young man, who took turns. They were both lovely but quite timid. We didn't feel like they belonged in the prison environment. One of the first prisons we went to, we were walking through the prison, towards the place where we were going to do the presentation, and there was a lot of shouting from the prisoners all around. This interpreter turned to us, a little embarrassed, and said to Ian, 'Do you want to know what they're saying?'

But Ian said, 'Nah, you're alright. I can probably imagine.'

However, when we got to the yard itself, where we were doing the presentation, and we set up and got the prisoners in, it was different. They loved watching the weights, and they listened quite attentively when we spoke. There were more than a hundred prisoners there, in this open-air yard, watching Joe squat and listening to Arf give testimony and me preach the gospel. There was a lot of response at the end.

It was the second meeting we did, at a different prison, that was very, very different. It was probably one of the only meetings I've ever done where I wasn't sure we would make it through. It was very, very edgy.

This establishment was a high-security place, so there were significant security checks, which made us feel a bit on edge even before we got in. It was me, Joe and Ian, and a couple of guys from the Christian group who had organised the trip.

They showed us into their gymnasium. It was a large concrete hut, really, in the middle of the prison complex; it was full of prisoners training, and they were massive! They were like extras from a Hollywood movie about hardcore East European gangsters. Big lumps with tattoos and shaved heads. Some of their equipment was quite primitive – it looked like debris left over from the First World War – axles, lumps of concrete, bits of metal.

There were two types of prison guard at this establishment. There were the regular guards, who were in uniform. They were the ones doing security at the entrance, and they were stationed in various places throughout the prison. However, when you got into the heart of the prison itself, there was a section of specialist high-security guards.

When we got into the gym, these high-security guards came in and stationed themselves around the room. Alarmingly, they were wearing balaclavas and body armour, and carrying machine guns. If you have guards like that, you know you've got serious violent inmates. We had been briefed about these guards at the prison entrance. Well, when I say 'briefed' . . . basically, someone had said, 'If anything kicks off, they will shoot you.'

Next thing we know, the guard who'd brought us in started telling all the prisoners to stop their training and come listen to us. That was *not* what they wanted to hear! They were seriously disgruntled. It's not as though they'd volunteered to come and hear us in a chapel service. It was just us walking in unannounced to their regular gym session, and interrupting fifty massive fellas in the middle of their workout. You don't really want to be doing that!

But he walked around, calling everyone off the equipment, then he disappeared, and there we were – Joe, Ian, me, a couple of Romanian Christians, two interpreters, some high-risk violent prisoners and a load of balaclava-wearing guards carrying machine guns.

We learned later that the reason those guards covered their faces was because they were members of the local community – often the same communities the prisoners came from – and if there was any trouble, they didn't want word getting out that it was them who shot this or that prisoner. So, they dressed like that – like terrorists – guns, balaclavas, stab vests, the lot.

And I know I've said it already, but these prisoners were enormous. Great hulking lumps of walking muscle with skinheads, or Mohicans, and a bad attitude. It was pretty uncomfortable. I wouldn't say we were afraid, but we could feel the danger, that's for sure. The whole time there was a heightened awareness of what might happen.

There was one prisoner who was clearly in charge. He was massive, tattooed all over, with a Mohican haircut. You could see that the others were taking their signal from him, and he was not too pleased to see us.

We tried to talk to the guy in charge through the interpreters, to introduce who we were and why we were there, but he was completely disinterested. It wasn't going anywhere.

So, I told Joe to start squatting . . .

We hadn't brought out own weights over to Romania, so we had bought some when we got there. We put a couple of weights on the bar, and Joe started squatting. The big guy was not impressed. You could have cut the tension with a knife. It was terrible. So Ian said to me, 'Stick on all the weight we've got.'

Ian

How the weights work is this: we generally have a PA and some music playing over the speakers. Whether it's in a church, a prison, on the streets, whatever. If we use the weights, we'll have a bit of music, which we turn down when we're giving testimony and turn up when we're lifting. We especially like to use the *Rocky* music. It gives that pumping, energetic feeling. Guys love it. If we do a competition for the crowd, it'll generally be the bench press, or the single log lift, but when we demonstrate lifting ourselves, it's the squats. The squat is where you can lift the maximum weight, because it's using your quad muscles, rather than primarily the arms. Arthur in his early days was regularly lifting 200kg with the squat.

We'll usually start with a low weight on the bars – 25kg on each end, for example, which is 70kg with the weight of the bar – and we'll do a few squats with that. Say it's Joe squatting, I'll be standing just behind him, encouraging him on: 'Come on, Joe! Keep it up, son!' I'll be spotting as well – keeping an eye that he doesn't overdo himself, helping put the weights back on the rack when he's done.

When he's done a few reps on the squats, we'll switch into someone's testimony – so, if it's Arf, he'll give the first section of his testimony – five minutes or so. While Arf is giving his story, Joe and I will stack a bit more weight on the ends of the bar. Then Arthur will break off his story, on a bit of a cliff-hanger, and we'll come back to the weights.

Joe will do another set of reps with the heavier weights on the bar, before going back to Arthur for the next part of his testimony.

This will repeat once or twice more, before we end with a maximum weight on the bar – probably 200kg or more. In a street presentation, I'll hype it up a bit: 'Look, we've got 200kg on there now! Let's see what Joe makes of that!'

But in a gym, you don't need to point that out. The guys can see what weight is being lifted, and they know how impressive that is.

Joe will do his last set of reps, right until he can't do any more, and we all give him a cheer, and then we go in with the gospel.

Arthur

So, back in this Romanian prison, we were not at all following the usual pattern of weights/testimony/weights/testimony. Joe and I loaded up the bar with pretty much everything we had, and we set him off squatting again. We probably stacked a good 200kg on that bar straight off, no building up to it.

Joe was fit but it was still a lot to ask, squatting that weight without warming up to it. You could see it was enormously heavy, but amazingly, he managed it. He properly delivered. He did a decent number of reps, and as he did them, you could see the prisoner with the Mohican sneering, but watching, and slowly his face changed. When Joe finished, he quietly nodded his respect for what had been lifted.

Ian

I remember whispering to Arf, 'Do your testimony. But make a big thing of your titles and trophies!'

I can't think of any other meeting where I've prayed so deliberately and intensely under my breath while Joe was lifting and while Arf was telling his testimony. Two or three of us from the group were bunched together just soaking the whole situation in prayer the whole way through.

We were really relying on the Holy Spirit to give us the words to say, inspire our timing and guide our actions. We'd had to be responsive, so we hadn't followed our usual formula, and there was this palpable tension.

I genuinely thought that either the guys were going to give up on us, go back to their training and we'd have to leave without saying our piece, or otherwise, that things would actually kick off – that these huge guys would set on us, and our only chance of getting out alive would be that the security guards would shoot the prisoners and not us.

It's not that you're afraid, but you do feel the danger and the physical vulnerability. You are confident, because you know that the Lord has sent you there, but the Lord hasn't necessarily promised to get you out again. You have decided to surrender to his will, whatever that might be. You can't assume anything. But amazingly, after Joe's squatting, there was a definite defrosting. I wouldn't say they were warm towards Arf, but they were listening. God was working.

By the time I got up to give the gospel, incredibly, we had them on our side.

I preached the gospel and by the end, the atmosphere was incredible. These guys were shaking our hands, giving us bear hugs, all of that. There was a language barrier, but I remember them tapping their chests, as if to say, 'You touched my heart.' It was brilliant.

The Lord really used the weights that day to calm things down and find a way through for us. He used Joe's fitness and strength to get their attention and a bit of respect. And off the back of that, we were able to give testimony and preach Jesus.

That was the last prison we went to in Romania, and we had no further use for the weights we'd bought, so we left them to the guys in that prison – an Olympic bar and a load of weights. We didn't want to take them home to England, and it was much better stuff than the homemade equipment they had there when we arrived – lumps of concrete, lumps of iron, old bars to bend. They had stuff in there that would have looked far-fetched even in the early *Rocky* movies.

That really blessed them, getting those weights. I like to think that whenever they used them, they remembered our testimony and the gospel of Jesus Christ.

Arthur

It's not about weights for their own sake. Otherwise, I'd be saying to everyone, 'If you want to evangelise, then get training so that you can powerlift at every event!' The point of the weights for us has been firstly, that they are a visual hook – they draw people in, give a point of reference and enable us to build rapport. We were at a youth meeting in Leeds, and I saw some young boys on their phones at the back, sitting there just scrolling and scrolling. But when Joe started lifting, they looked up.

Secondly, they are genuinely part of our story. I was a powerlifter, Joe was a powerlifter, and Ian was a bodybuilder. So, the weights aren't a gimmick. They are a relevant way of pointing to our stories – to what God has done in our lives. If you've been a dancer, do a dance. If you're an artist, paint a picture. Whatever you do – balloon-modelling, card tricks, or bridge-building demonstrations – God can use it to connect with people. It can say something truthful about you that then leads into your testimony. God uses what you've got in your hands. Whatever it is he's already given you – a talent or ability, some resources, your personality and character – that's what God will use to bring people to himself.

Thirdly, God has used the weights to connect with certain groups of men that other things don't connect with. Over and over again we meet men who say, 'I thought Christians were all wimps.' And seeing us has shifted their perception. Suddenly, from watching Joe lift weights, they find they're listening to me tell how God saved me from crime and steroid abuse. From there, they're listening to Ian while he explains the saving grace of God – how God didn't leave us alone in this world, but was interested enough to come himself, in the form of the man Jesus, to die and get back the relationship between humans and God that was meant to be there from the beginning.

So, the weights have got us accepted into all sorts of places where we would never imagine we could get an invite, and where we would not have been listened to without them. God's used the lifting to take Tough Talk to a lot of places that other people don't go. Prisons are a case in point, especially outside the UK. Who would go there? What would they say?

How would they start? It's the weights that God has used to open those doors for us.

Ian

There are a few moments when the weights have created some chaos. We had a funny incident when we went on a mission to Texas years back – that was me, Joe, Adam and one other. We didn't take our own weights, but we had decided to take our own squat stands over on the plane. We wrapped them up in bubble wrap, and we checked them in as oversized luggage.

We got to Texas, and touched down. We all went off to baggage reclaim, and everyone was standing there waiting for the luggage to come off the plane.

We were waiting and waiting. No one's luggage was coming out. Everyone was getting het-up. It was about an hour waiting for our luggage. Everyone was questioning what was going on. People were moaning. Some were trying to find some crew or staff to explain what was going on.

Slowly, the conveyor belt started creaking into action. Everyone's eyes snapped to where the luggage would be coming out, but all that appeared was a bra. Then a pair of knickers. Then some other pieces of clothing and underwear, snagged and torn. Then a couple of damaged cases, spilling their contents.

Then, from the same place as this trickle of luggage debris, an airport worker came walking up the conveyor belt, looking pretty unamused with the whole situation, and he was holding one of our squat stands in each hand.

He stood up on the luggage reclaim, and loudly said to everyone, 'Whoever owns these, you can blame *them* for the delay!' And he chucked our squat stands onto the conveyor with distaste.

Then the carousel started up properly, and all this luggage started coming up, and it was carnage! All the cases were open. There were clothes spilling out, there were pants and bras and ripped jackets and shirts in tatters. Not only had our squat stands jammed the system, they'd somehow caused everything else to get chewed up in it as well.

At this point, the passengers were absolutely fuming, and I remember whispering to Joe, 'Let's not go and get those stands right now, eh?' and Joe nodded, and we tried to look inconspicuous. We stood there trying to look casual until everyone else had taken their luggage off. We had Adam with us – Adam is always so willing – and eventually I said,

'Adam, in a little while, when no one's looking, nip round and pick those stands up for us, will ya?'

It wasn't even our fault. We had said they were oversized, and someone had gone and put them in with all the other luggage. But there was no way I wanted a barrage of fuming Texans coming at me in the airport, so we nipped over when everyone else had gone, and reclaimed our squat stands. And that was the start of our Texan mission!

Arthur

The lifting has been, in many ways, the most unique part of Tough Talk, but it could have become a weight around our neck – so to speak – if we had let it.

Now that we're getting a bit older, there's still some emphasis on the weights, but the fact is, we can't lift what we used to, and it's a long time since any of us were champions or record holders, so that whole thing is a bit less relevant. We still do the lifting, the weights, the competitions for the crowd, because it's who we are, we love it and it gets people's interest. But we don't do it at every single meeting or occasion. It's much more important to us that we are always telling people about Jesus.

One of the things I'm proud of Tough Talk for is that we haven't relied on the weights more than we should. Even when the weights were a big thing, they were never the biggest thing. They were never the purpose of what we did. The weights always pointed to testimony, and the testimony always pointed to the gospel. The weights by themselves are pointless.

Ian

If you take away the gospel, then the testimony is an interesting story that happened to somebody else, but doesn't become personally relevant to the listener. If you take away the testimony, then the weights are fun and a bit of a sideshow, but don't actually have any relevance or meaning.

A man we met had invited his son to come to an event we were running at a local church. He'd shown his son the flier, with pictures of us and the weights on it, and the son had apparently said, 'Church is becoming more and more like a pantomime – no wonder nobody's going!'

Well, actually, I get that. I don't want to go to church and see a pantomime either. We are not there for entertainment. If you go to church, you want to get some kind of eternally relevant message. Something meaty. So, I kind of agree with his comment, even though I could have taken offence. I mean, if you want to see a pantomime, go to the theatre! But if he had come, I don't think he would have seen a pantomime. He would have seen a visually interesting, dynamic presentation which led on to personal stories, which then gave way to an explanation of the power of God to save even the most vicious sinner when he repents and turns from his own way, and puts his life in Jesus' hands.

That is actually what we are all about.

> Even if I walk through a valley as dark as the grave, I will
> not be afraid of any danger, because you are with me.
> Your rod and staff comfort me.
>
> *Ps. 23:4–5, ESV*

Chapter Sixteen

On the Road

> The joy of the Lord is your strength.
>
> *Neh. 8:10, NKJV*

Arthur

From the first time I met Ian, he was running a prayer meeting from his office on a Tuesday night. It was an important element of the ministry, getting the Tough Talk guys together regularly to pray and be accountable to each other. You don't go out on the road – into the battle – without bringing everything to God.

When I had a leg operation and couldn't get out, they started coming round to my house, also east London/Essex way. We would cook up some chicken and rice, eat in the kitchen, then go through to the lounge for a bit of prayer and worship. We had some great meetings together. It was safe, it was honest and it was manly. We'd all been through traumas in life – marital traumas included. We could talk about anything, give honest feedback to each other, and we all grew through it.

Jacqui would sit in the back room of our house, and she will tell you she sometimes used to cry with joy at the sound of us men singing and praying together.

It's nothing special. We were not super-spiritual, and we certainly weren't great singers, but we were men together praising the Lord and fellowshipping. We all need that, yet it's surprisingly unusual for guys.

There was one time my son, James, had a friend coming over on a Tuesday evening. James got a phone call. It was his mate, saying, 'I've been ringing your doorbell, but no one's answering, it's so noisy! What's going on in there?'

James said, 'Oh, that's just my dad's prayer meeting!'

Then for a time we had an office round my church, so we held the prayer meeting there. Then Jacqui and I moved to Cornwall, and we started holding it on Zoom, which we still do now. It's still a highlight of the week. Prayer holds everything together, and being together in God's presence creates a deep friendship that sustains us all.

Fellowship's important. We joke with each other and have a laugh, but I can put my hand on my heart and say, 'I know Ian's here for me.' And I know that Ian can say the same for me, and the same with Joe and the other guys who meet with us from time to time.

In Proverbs it says, 'As one piece of iron sharpens another, so friends keep each other sharp' (Prov. 27:17, ERV). That is how I would describe us three, because we talk honestly. Our hearts are all focused on Jesus.

When Ian picks me up in the van for an event, or when we pick up Joe, we'll have a bit of a catch-up. We might talk about our families, maybe five minutes about cars, or sport, or how the training's going. Then the rest of the time we talk about Jesus. Hours and hours in the car, we talk about the Bible and our lives and God.

There was discipline in my life when I was competing. I was disciplined about my training, my diet and my lifestyle. Now it's the same with my Christian life – I'm reading the Bible, praying and witnessing. You've got to have those three things.

Before we go out witnessing, we get praying and we get reading the Word together. There's no point sitting vegging out, watching rubbish on TV. You want to be reading the Word, talking to your brothers and sisters and praying together. That is your spiritual training, your physical maintenance regime. You want to be sharp. The more you put these disciplines into practice in your life the better. There are fewer doors for the devil to get in.

Ian and I have driven four hours from Essex to Liverpool, done a forty-five-minute meeting, then got in the van and driven back that same night. You tell anyone you're doing that – without being paid – and they will say, 'You're bonkers!' Maybe it is bonkers! But it's what we do, what we want to do, and what we believe God wants us doing.

The truth is, that short time you're there at the meeting might actually be an incredibly important moment for people. You might touch eternity in that short time. So, we do it, and we keep on doing it.

Ian

I'm sure some people think we're mad just for the logistics, because it does impose on your personal life, your home life. You can't go to all the church events – you can't even get to church a lot of Sundays. You can't promise your wife you'll always be around on a Thursday evening, or whatever it might be. But when you're out there and somehow – despite the traffic, despite the problems, despite whatever else is going on at home, you arrive on time, when it didn't look like you'd ever arrive; when suddenly the PA is working when it looked like it wasn't going to work; when the meeting suddenly starts to fill up, when it looked like nobody was coming, and then you feel the life of God flowing through you, and you have the opportunity to speak the truth of God, to tell the story of his power in your life and to pray for someone – the joy is incredible.

To stand there with God as your passport – some ordinary, not particularly clever bloke suddenly making a difference in someone's life and bringing glory to God, that's what excites me and keeps me going.

The great thing is, Arf, Joe and me, we share that. It brings us alive. People say to Arf, 'You must be exhausted,' but actually Jacqui says that when he comes home from a mission, he's more energised than ever. He's moving in the fullness of who God made him to be.

There's not a lot of glamour on the road with Tough Talk, but there is a lot of joy. Arthur and I went on a mission to various prisons around 1999/2000, and Steve came with us, who was part of Tough Talk at the time.

They'd arranged for us to stay in a monastery. It was a long train journey, then we got a taxi, and were dropped at this place in the pitch dark. It was pouring with rain and the wind was howling, and they dropped us at the front of this old, gothic monastery, in the pitch dark. There was no one there. It was pretty spooky.

We pushed open this big, creaky door – it was like a set from a horror movie – and went inside. There were little notes, a sort of trail of them, telling us what to do. They told us where to find our rooms for sleeping – 'cells' of course, being a monastery – we had one each – and there were notes in the kitchen telling us where the breakfast was. The building was full of stone statues of saints, it felt like they were watching us.

In the morning, after we'd left the monastery, Steve told us that after going into his bedroom, he had pushed his wardrobe in front of the door, just in case . . .

Arthur

Sometimes it's lonely because we do stuff alone a lot of the time, as well as events in twos and threes. It's hard. I'm not saying it's harder than being a pastor or than other people's lives or anything. It's just different.

It's the travel that does me in. I'll be up from 4 a.m. till 10 p.m. at night, for the sake of a couple of sessions forty-five minutes long. You're not sure what you've eaten or what you're doing next, or what exactly has been achieved. Often my legs are aching; I may have left before my wife was up, and she'll have gone to bed by the time I get home. It is really for no gain, except for Christ. We would not do it for any other reason. Obviously. It would be a nonsense. We would not do it if we weren't totally, constantly focused on the cross.

I've got zero interest in boasting in myself, or even in Ian. I'm proud of Tough Talk. Like Paul, we can stand up and say, we're 'not ashamed of the gospel . . . for it is the power of God to salvation for everyone who believes' (Rom. 1:16, NKJV).

Our focus is nothing but glorifying Christ – talking about what he's done in our lives, and through that, bringing other people into his truth. Our old mate Adam used to pray, 'Lord, let us be nameless and faceless!' He wasn't a big one for words of wisdom, but that one always stuck with me. There's no need for people to remember us, or what we look like, or what we say. It's not to do with us, it's the Lord.

Ian

I don't think we have ever turned down a gig. Nothing's too small. If someone invites us, off we go. I remember vividly, we once did a presentation at the Manchester City stadium. It was part of a huge Christmas event, being recorded by BBC television. It was presented by Don Maclean, the comedian who was originally on *Crackerjack*, and there were loads of other celebrities there, with about 20–25,000 people in the audience. The next day out in Essex, we did a Boys' Brigade meeting with about ten kids there. And really for us, there's no difference. God is interested in every single person.

There are some things that are logistically or practically impossible, but we've never turned things down for any other reason. In fact, once or twice, we've been somewhere, and the organisers have said, 'Look, there's almost nobody here. Shall we call if off?' But we've said, 'No, we're here, let's just get on with it.'

I work with the Probation Office sometimes in Leeds, and I know it will be a small number of people, but it doesn't matter. You're going there for God. I mean, you don't take a big group of men and weights and all that, but you still do it. You respect the invitation and the individuals. We just go where we are invited.

Arthur

We did a mission in Scotland many years ago. A Baptist church contacted us, and from the off he was honest about it. He said, 'We're very small, just one or two families. I can't afford to give you anything, but would you come and speak?' It really was a tiny little church. We had some lunch, and did our presentation to the couple of families who were there. We'd lined it up to fit in with another mission we were doing in another part of Scotland, so that was fine. I don't think we've ever turned anything down except for double bookings, or something that's genuinely logistically impossible.

Ian

There was that earlier phase, where we were this looser group of a larger number of blokes. There were guys who were kind of with us, but they wouldn't sign up for many events, or they would sign up and then not turn up, or something. It was frustrating! You can encourage people, but either you're up for it or you're not, and I really don't want to be dragging people, that is just too much effort.

We ended up having too many personalities involved, then their wives get involved, everyone suddenly had all sorts of opinions on all sorts of issues, and to be honest, I've not got the patience for things like that. It's not my strength. I just wanted to get on with preaching the gospel.

Me and Arf, we've really hardly had any arguments at all, over these thirty years. Honestly, barely a cross word. We haven't fallen out. Joe as well. A couple of times in the early days, we both pulled Joe into line, but that was fine – he responded well, he sorted himself out and he's stuck with us. He's amazing to work with because he's committed like we are.

So, life is a bit easier now, with the three of us forming the main core of Tough Talk. That suits me and it suits the organisation. There are a few guys who will still come out with us every so often, and that is great. We love seeing these characters turn up when we are near their home, or their church, or working with an organisation they are involved in. That works well.

If I turn round and say we're doing something in west London – Kensington Temple, or in my own stomping ground – Ilford, east London – I will always get a few lads put their hands up, and that is brilliant.

Of course, if I announced that we were going on a mission to the south of Spain for a week, I'd have plenty of volunteers! But like I said, it's not usually that glamorous!

Arthur

Either Ian rings me and says, 'Can you do Bristol last weekend in May?' or whatever it is. Or I just ring Ian and say,

'What you got coming up, mate?' and we go through the calendar. That's how it goes. Ian's in charge of organising most things, but quite a few of the invitations come to me, or through me. Sometimes I go somewhere on my own, down near home. Ian has a number of things he does on his own, like Teen Challenge, and often he and Joe go together somewhere, particularly if it's their area of the country more than mine. But you don't feel like one person's putting most of the effort in. It's very much energy from all of us.

It has to be a priority. You have to decide to make it a big thing in your life. Of course, it depends on your family situation. Ian's and my kids have long left home, whereas Joe still has a youngish family, and he has a full-time job as well. But the thing is, he has the commitment, and he works very hard for Tough Talk around the other things in his life.

Powerlifting is a very individual sport. I trained alone, I competed alone. So now, being in a team with Tough Talk, I love it.

Ian

The joy of the Lord has to be your strength.[1] That's the key.

I mean, be real, but don't spend the time moaning and groaning. I couldn't do a ten-hour journey with Arthur if he was just talking about his health, and moaning about how awful it was. No. We ask each other how we are, he gives me an update. He doesn't fake anything – he tells me honestly what's going on, and then we move on. We talk about westerns for ten minutes and then we talk about the things of the gospel.

If we turn up somewhere and the bed's rotten, the wind's howling, the room's freezing cold, we've learned not to moan about it. I might say to Arf, 'It's proper grim, mate!' But then we'll both get on with life. We try and follow in the footsteps of the old missionaries and evangelists – if we're given a bed, we'll sleep in a bed. If we're not given a bed, we'll sleep on the floor, but whatever happens, we'll be joyful that we're serving the Lord.

I'm not being unrealistic, or suggesting we pretend we're happy when we're not. Life on the road can be painful, in a lot of different ways. But if you look within yourself with self-pity and say, 'Woe is me,' you're going nowhere. If you look up and say, 'Praise the Lord. I live for you, God,' then you will be open to living in the joy of the Lord. That's been my decision. Whatever happens, whether I'm comfortable or not, whether I live or not, I'm going to be his, and I'm going to live for him. So, joy becomes one of the weapons in your spiritual battle.

I think of that time in the Philippines when I woke up and was moaning to myself, grumbling about the state of the room, the lumps in the mattress, the dirty floor, all the traffic and car horns beeping outside all night long. Then a few hours later we went into that prison, and we saw those poor, half-alive souls in their cells, smothered in excrement, nothing to lie down on, looking like they'd not had a meal since yesterday's breakfast. And it taught me a lesson, which is never to grumble.

Arthur

I've heard Ian's and Joe's stories a million times, I've said my own a million times, and yet it still fires me up to hear what God has done in our lives.

We were talking a while ago about some of the things we'd gone through. Me with my heart and my operations, my pain and lack of energy, and Ian with his business issues and personal issues and all sorts, and Ian said, 'We've just got to focus on Jesus and the cross.'

You listen to someone like Billy Graham, and that's what comes through – it's all about Jesus and the cross. That is our first priority.

You need to seek those people out who will say, 'Hallelujah, praise the Lord.' Not in a fake way, but in a committed way, because we believe in a God who is so much bigger than every circumstance. We believe in an eternity that is so much more real than this earth.

The only time I'll stop is if I'm physically incapable of doing it any more. Or if Ian takes me aside and says, 'Arf, you're finished. Time to stop. That's four times in one week you've fallen off the front of the platform and taken out a nice lady in the front row. I can't keep picking you up off the ground. You've gotta call it a day, mate!'

Ian

The cost of following Christ is a large part of our faith. Jesus challenges the disciples in strong words. When he says, 'Follow Me, and let the dead bury their own dead' or 'take up [your] cross daily' or – to the rich young ruler – 'sell whatever you have . . . and come . . . follow Me' (Matt. 8:22; Luke 9:23; Mark 10:21, NKJV), he's basically saying, if you can't give up everything else compared to following me, then you're not with me.

Missionary David Livingstone went out to the jungle, and he gave his whole life to it. He didn't go for a week. He went with the attitude that he was going to live there and die there. I think he barely saw a single convert in his life – but look at his legacy.[2] Eric Liddell stayed in China when Britain told all its nationals to leave. He served the people of China, and he died in a Japanese internment camp.[3] Missionaries in Hudson Taylor's day, they packed their stuff up in a coffin and off they went – because they knew that was the only thing they would come back in. That was the mindset; extraordinary devotion and belief in the value of what you were doing. You didn't expect to see instant results. It wasn't like a gap year. It was for life, and that was the cost.[4]

Arthur

It's hard and it's hard work. Of course. But I've never felt like chucking it in. I've been discouraged. Occasionally it's been so hard I've sat there in tears, wondering what's going on. If you were doing it for recognition, or prizes, or money, or whatever, of course you would give it up. It makes no sense. But with Christ in your life, and the focus on the cross, you have that eternal perspective.

There was a funny moment in South Africa one time. We were staying in this quite nice hotel for a change, and we went for a meal in their restaurant, and there was another Brit there, having a meal, and of course you notice someone who is obviously foreign, and we said, 'Hello, mate, how you doing?'

It turned out he was there to play golf. I don't know if he was with his wife, or his girlfriend, or what. But he was playing golf out there, and then he asked me, 'What are you doing?'

So, we told him: 'We flew out here yesterday, we're here going into a prison this morning, preaching about God, then into a school tomorrow, then another prison, then we're flying home that evening.' And he just could not get his head round why two blokes would fly all that way to not go and see anything! To be fair, we saw Table Mountain from the car going to and from the airport, and the ocean, and we could see that it was a really beautiful place. But that's not what we were there for.

We've done a couple of trips to South Africa, and both times we flew out Thursday night from Heathrow or Gatwick to Cape Town overnight, and got there on Friday morning. We went straight into schools on Friday, prisons at the weekend, and got the plane home Sunday night. People thought we were absolutely bonkers, with that intensity of travel and no time off for sightseeing. But our thinking is, we can do a lot of work, see a lot of people, in three or four days – we can give people a message that might affect their eternal destiny. Let's make the most of it.

Don't get me wrong, we do go on holidays. But we make it a thing that when we're on a mission, we treat that like business, so we seldom do any sightseeing. It's just the way me, Ian and Joe work best – to keep that focus.

People can be surprised, or think we're crazy, or even criticise as much as they like. But what we've done is stuck to what God has led us to. And we know that God has impacted many, many people through the work we have done.

I mean, people have literally told me I'm mad, because I'll get on a train at 6 a.m. at Bodmin, go into London, go to Pentonville prison, do our thing, address a load of prisoners, get on a train again and be home past midnight. People are like, 'Why would you do that?'

Well, the answer, obviously, is that Jesus Christ changed my life, and I want to let other people have a chance to meet him as well. As long as I can stand – or be propped up – or sit in a chair and tell people how amazing my Jesus is, that's what I'll be doing.

The joy of the LORD will make you strong.

Neh. 8:10, ERV

Chapter Seventeen

Fathers, Grandfathers and the Name of Jesus

Therefore God also has highly exalted Him and given Him
the name which is above every name,
that at the name of Jesus every knee should bow, of those
in heaven, and of those on earth, and of those under the
earth, and that every tongue should confess that Jesus
Christ is Lord, to the glory of God the Father.

Phil. 2:9–11, NKJV

Arthur

Someone said to me once, 'You can't do youth work any more.'

I said, 'Why is that?'

'Well,' he said, 'you know, trying to be young, at your age –
it's not going to work, is it?'

That's nonsense.

We're not trying to be young, and if we were, that would
be a disaster anyway. We're being ourselves. And young people
respond to that. Besides, in the youth world, once you're in
your thirties, you're 'old'!

If we were turning up in trendy jeans, with razor cuts in our hair or whatever, trying to fit the image, that would be ridiculous. But we're not. We're going in with who we are. At the end of the day, I'm an old man with a life story, and actually, the kids love it when I stand up and say, 'I'm the grandad in the team!'

They see my grey hair, and my grey handlebar moustache, and then they see that I'm wearing a bomber jacket or a hoodie and I've got heavy black boots on and they really connect. They like that individuality. I've been welcomed and applauded in many schools, simply because I've been myself and told my own story, and they relate to that.

My conversion story is a long way in the past now. It's more than thirty years since that happened. But my life with Jesus is happening right now! So I'll talk about being a grandad and believing in God, and explain how I first came to Christ.

We went to Liverpool once, and we were talking to some youth workers afterwards, and they mentioned that a lot of these kids have got no father figure or even grandfather figure in their lives. They don't understand that relationship. So that alone is appealing for them. The idea that an older person is interested in you, and might have some wisdom about life, might have stories that could inspire you – that is great. The Bible says we have many instructors in Christ, but not many fathers.[1] It's talking about spiritual fathers, but there's a wider truth there, which is that we all need parent figures in our lives.

Ian

Sometimes I think it's quite funny, really, how us two old codgers go into schools and talk to these young people.

Back in 2023 or so, Arf was speaking, giving his testimony to 1,000 kids in a school assembly, and I could see he was looking for something to lean on. All the time I've known Arf, he's been a pacer – while he's talking, he walks up and down, up and down. Nowadays, he can't do that quite as well – there's a limit to how long he can march up and down; he does have to stop sometimes, and talk while he's leaning on the back of a chair, or something like that.

So we were at this school, and I could tell, in-between talking, that Arf was kind of trying to find something to rest against, and then he saw the PA kit. So, he's coming to the PA, and just resting his back on this big black speaker box that's set up by the side of the stage in the assembly hall. But he hadn't given the box much of a look, and the box was on wheels!

I'm listening to Arthur give his testimony, and I'm over the other side of the platform, so I can't sort of subtly stick my foot behind the back wheel to stop it rolling, or anything like that. So, I'm just thinking, 'Lord, please don't let him lean any harder on that speaker, because if he does, those wheels will start rolling, and Arthur and the PA and the microphone and everything else will disappear off the back of the platform, in front of 1,000 kids.' Thankfully, that isn't how it ended, praise the Lord!

The point is, we're not young. We're both grandparents – in fact, I've got more grandchildren than Arf has, even though I'm fifteen years younger. But I truly believe it's God's grace on us, that we can stand in front of condemned men, and preach a gospel of hope, then stand in front of kids just starting out their lives and preach the same gospel of hope.

Arthur

It's the way that God's opened doors for us that still blows my mind. We'll be in a prison one minute, in a drug rehab the next, and then we'll go and do a school meeting where we've got all these little kids listening. Sometimes I almost can't believe the range of places that God has taken us to speak his Word.

I don't think you can put us in one box and say, 'This is what Tough Talk do, and this is where they do it.' I wouldn't ever want to be in that box anyway. We speak about our own lives, and we preach the gospel. Sometimes we lift weights. That's our gift, our calling, our ministry, whatever you want to call it; that's how God has decided he's going to work through us. But he's done it in all sorts of places, with all sorts of people, in all sorts of ways that we never would have imagined.

I went to New York on my own in early 2001, to do some preparations for a third visit later that year. One of the places I went was a New York Police Department precinct. I'd been invited to speak there, at the point where they all come together in the morning and the sergeant gives out the orders for the day. It wasn't much different to *Hill Street Blues*! There were a couple of hundred officers all lined up in their blue uniforms, their hats and NYPD badges, before going out on the early morning shift. I remember standing there thinking I was on a film set, or in a telly programme. I said to the sergeant, 'What shall I say?' and she said, 'Just tell 'em.'

I gave a testimony and brought a gospel message, and then the sergeant, at the end, said, 'Shall we pray, then?'

So, we prayed. I led these 200 police officers in a prayer for God's blessing. It was almost surreal. I just thought, 'Lord, this is you. There's no way I could have made this happen.'

Ian

After the prison in the Philippines, we went to a high school. It wasn't far away, maybe a mile or so, but we needed to take the van to transport the gym equipment. So, some of us walked, some drove. We left at the same time, and the guys who walked got there before us!

The schools there are amazing. The kids are smartly dressed. Discipline's important. They're full of respect and good behaviour. They don't take education for granted like we do here – they respect it, they know it's an opportunity.

The school meeting was a good one. It was packed – quite a few hundred kids. There's a lot of faith there already, it's a very Christian country, so you've got permission to be open with the gospel. In fact, you're respected for being a Christian – and they want you to go for it. They would see us as Christian ministers, so we were already held in high regard. I got a letter from a local civic leader afterwards saying how wonderful it was to have us there, and what a great job we had done preaching to the children. I'd never get that back home!

When we're invited to schools in the UK, the Christian teacher or chaplain inviting us will quite often be a bit nervous about how we are going to present our faith. They might have seen us at a church event and booked us on the back of that, but they need to know that we're going to tailor our approach when we come into their school. They need to know that we understand their position, and won't do anything to jeopardise it.

So, in the Philippines, when they said to us, 'Go for it, preach the gospel!' it was a shock! We did preach the gospel, and the children were very responsive and bowed their heads and prayed along with us at the end.

On one of our trips to New York, we had a big debate. We were preparing to go into a school, and suddenly we were told that we were not allowed to say the word 'Jesus'. We were allowed to say 'God' but not 'Jesus'. We had this big discussion. Shall we go in? Should we not? There was quite a big team of us – five or six blokes. Some wanted to go in anyway, and some didn't.

While we were discussing it, one of them looked down at our squat stands and saw we had the words, 'Soldiers for Christ' written on them, and somehow that clinched it for us. We just thought, when they see the word 'Christ' on our squat stands, they're going to know, when we talk about God, which God we're talking about.

It was the discussion that was so interesting, though – asking ourselves, 'What's the purpose of us going in there if we can't speak about Jesus Christ and him crucified?' I've got nothing to offer those kids if I can't tell them that Jesus – the Son of God – died for their sins.

Arthur

Actually, there was a strong Christian element in that school already. We got quite a few 'Amens' from the kids as we spoke, so we knew we were making ourselves clear.

The funny thing was, afterwards, the principal of the school invited us to come back, and this time to share the gospel. So, once they had seen us, and seen that we weren't nutcases, they wanted us back, and they were open to our message. We couldn't go back, actually, because of our schedule – but we would have otherwise.

There are rules and regulations and expectations in Western schools. You don't want to upset that, and you don't want to wreck things for the Christian staff who are there, who have invited you. But, if you've built a relationship, shown someone that you're an authentic person, a normal person with a genuine religious or supernatural experience – not some crazy guy or con artist – then there is a real acceptance. We have actually found, quite often, that staff who are not Christian will say, 'Go for it, tell it all, say what you like,' especially if they have seen us before, and therefore have some trust in who we are and how we conduct ourselves.

Tough Talk has got a bit of a reputation, actually, for talking a lot about Jesus. Now, that sounds silly, for a Christian evangelistic charity – but you'd be surprised how reluctant even Christians can be to use the name of Jesus. Yet, it's the most powerful name. So, I'm proud to say that we speak about Jesus.

Ian

The Lord has given us the ability to do this whole variety of scenarios. Early on, I found myself speaking at a police carol service, with 500 coppers standing in front of me fully uniformed. I remember thinking, 'I need to word this the right way to not get nicked at the end of the conversation – I wonder if anyone's still got anything on me . . . '

Sometimes, the police are some of the most sceptical listeners, because they don't believe that people can change. So, it was good to stand there and give testimony that God had turned my life around.

Arthur

The Lord has got us into a ridiculous range of places – I've stood in front of army battalions and naval cadets, in front of criminals and schoolchildren, I'm spoken with drug addicts, homeless men, businessmen and Christian leaders. Once we got into an extremely posh private school and gave an assembly, on the basis of our powerlifting background and weights demonstration. We certainly wouldn't have got in there for any social or educational reason!

Ian

The fact is, God uses us where and how he wants to. It's up to him. And where he calls us, he equips us.

I was at a prison in 2023, and did a load of meetings, and at the end, the chaplain said to me, 'Can you spare twenty minutes to talk to my son?' His teenage son had got himself into a bit of trouble, and was in quite a fix. I sat and chatted to the fella. I gave him my testimony book, shared with him about my life a bit, and said, 'Let's pray together – God can sort this out.' So we prayed, and the boy was in tears by the end. When I left, the chaplain told me I had an incredible ability to connect with people.

I shook my head. 'Well, you know, that can only be God.'

I'm not that person. I'm not naturally drawn to relate one-on-one, or counsel people. I'm happier up the front. I'm not socially geared up. My wife still regularly prods me just to go and say hello to someone we know in a café or whatever. When the chaplain asked me to speak to his son, to be honest, I would much rather have got in the car and gone home.

If I thought I was there in my own strength, I'd be doubting myself. I'd be thinking, 'Does this lad really want to hear from me?' But the Lord wanted me to be there for that moment, for that purpose, for that specific individual. I did it in his strength, and for his sake.

> So God raised him up to the most important place and gave him the name that is greater than any other name. God did this so that every person will bow down to honor the name of Jesus. Everyone in heaven, on earth, and under the earth will bow. They will all confess, 'Jesus Christ is Lord,' and this will bring glory to God the Father.
>
> *Phil. 2:9–11,* ERV

Chapter Eighteen

Who Do You Say I Am?

> [Jesus] said to them, 'But who do you say that I am?'
> Simon Peter answered and said, 'You are the Christ, the Son of the living God.'
> Jesus answered and said to him, 'Blessed are you, Simon Bar-Jonah, for flesh and blood has not revealed this to you, but My Father who is in heaven.'
>
> *Matt. 16:15–17, NKJV*

Ian

One thing that has changed very significantly within the ministry's time, over these thirty years, is the rise of Islam in the UK. There was a time when I barely encountered any Muslims at all. Yet now, we meet Muslims everywhere we work – in streets ministry, in schools and particularly in prisons. Some of them are Muslims by birth, some are converts.

Twenty years ago, I was invited to speak in a girls' school in east London, which was 99 per cent Muslim. They had various faith assemblies, which the girls could choose to go to or not. A young woman from a Christian schools' organisation in Newham was taking the Christian assemblies, and she was really good at it. She made it fun and sang songs and her assemblies became really popular. She used to get 100 or 200 girls in. They would come in with their Islamic dress, wearing their head coverings, and they'd enjoy themselves in these Christian assemblies. She got me in to give testimony and share the gospel, and that's when I really started to realise that I hadn't given evangelism with Muslims much thought.

At the beginning, I kind of thought to myself, 'If I can just share my testimony, they're going to think, "Wow, this is the true God!"', which was pretty naïve, to be honest. I didn't realise that it was far more complex than that. As I encountered more and more Muslims and started to talk to them about all sorts of issues, I realised that I needed to shift my perspective and understanding if I wanted to make any sense at all as a Christian wanting to share the gospel.

Firstly, I had to realise that for many Muslims I was meeting, Islam wasn't just their religion or faith. It was their culture, their family, their lifestyle, their politics, their whole world. They didn't separate what they believed from their culture, nationality, family and so on – it was all very meshed together. In a similar way, Muslims who have come to the UK from other countries will often perceive that people here are all Christians, because that's the history of our culture. They think it's still a Christian country. So, you can understand it when they look around at people in the UK, and how they are living, and think, 'Wow, these Christians are really immoral.'

Secondly, for Christians going out evangelising in this country, the majority of the time, we'll start by trying to persuade someone that there is a God. Lots of people are atheists, even more are agnostic. With Islam, it's not about starting with 'There is a God'. That's a given – it's a shared assumption. However, once you start talking about Jesus, it's very, very different.

As an evangelical and Pentecostal myself, I've heard people get really excited because they have been talking to a Muslim about Jesus, and the Muslim has said, 'Oh yes, I love Jesus,' and they feel they're making some progress. The problem is, it's not the Jesus you're thinking of.

Muslims believe in Jesus. He's in the Quran. They believe he existed on earth, he was a prophet, and they're told to love him. In their scriptures, Jesus is called the Word of God.[1] He is called the spirit of God,[2] he is born of a virgin[3] and he is called the Messiah.[4] But they do not believe that he died, or rose again. Their texts say it was made to look like Jesus died on the cross – that the god of the Quran deceived all Christians into thinking that Jesus was crucified.[5] The same passage says that one of the twelve disciples was put on the cross instead of Jesus at the last moment. So, they believe that Jesus never died. They think he was taken up into heaven like Enoch or Elijah, and that he's still alive, at the right hand of God.

They do not believe Jesus was God's Son. In the Quran and Hadith, God isn't a father, and he has no son. This is a key part of their basic understanding of God. It's in the daily chants and prayers of their faith. Whereas for Christians, Jesus is fundamentally God's 'only begotten Son' (John 3:16, NKJV) – that's a very, very key part of our faith. Yet often, we Christians will talk about Jesus as though there is a universal view of who he is. That's wrong. A Muslim viewpoint very much includes Jesus, but sees him very differently.

A friend of mine who is a mum was talking to a grandmother in a toddler group, and the grandmother was a Muslim.

They were talking about faith, and suddenly this Muslim lady said, 'How can you believe in Christianity when you don't even know when Jesus was born? We know exactly when the Prophet was born, but you don't even know Jesus' birthday.'

My friend was taken by surprise. It had never occurred to her that knowing a date of birth could be important, and she felt like this lovely grandmother, who was a friend of hers, was suddenly laughing at her faith because of this particular detail. She didn't know how to respond to that point, which to her was completely unexpected. They kept talking about their children, grandchildren and everything else. But they didn't talk about faith again.

So, in all these things, there is the appearance of common ground, but there are enormous divergences of thinking, and this can be really deceptive and confusing if you're not expecting it. If you don't have a basic understanding of the Islamic perspective, it is going to be very difficult to effectively share the gospel with a Muslim.

The doctrine of the Trinity is another example. If you are a Christian, and someone mentions the Trinity, you will be thinking about the three-in-one God, who is Father, Son and Holy Spirit – one God, existing in three co-equal, co-eternal persons – three persons sharing one substance and nature. But when Muslims hear the word 'Trinity,' they think of God the Father, Mary the mother of Jesus and Jesus the Son, because that's what's in their texts about Christianity. And to them, that is blasphemous, because it's about Mary and God the Father having sex together to produce Jesus the Son.

So, when we're sharing our faith with Muslims, and we go about using phrases like 'God . . . sent his only begotten Son' (1 John 4:9, NKJV), or 'the Trinity', there is a whole different thought process going on in their minds, and if you don't understand that, they are going to think you are talking blasphemy and crazy talk.

Another major point of difference is that when you are talking to a non-religious person about your faith, there's a single direction to it. You are explaining your faith, and you are wanting to increase their understanding, and persuade them to investigate. When you talk to a Muslim about your faith, you will generally find that it's two-way. They will want to explain their faith to you, and want you to feel that their faith is something you need to investigate. What's more, they might be well prepared – even trained – to try and make you doubt your own faith, and dismantle your beliefs. I think Christians really need to realise this, and be ready for it, or the rug can properly get pulled from under them.

The term for the Muslim equivalent of evangelism is *dawah*. It means an invitation or a summons to worship. Some schools of thought will teach Muslims how to have polemics against Christianity. They will learn to use specific Bible passages – out of context – to try to disprove Christianity, or to catch Christians off guard. They will ask strawman questions – curve-ball questions – based around putting you off track and making you feel uncertain about your beliefs. If you're aware of this, you are less likely to be floored by it.

So, to go back to the Trinity, a Muslim might say to you that the Bible contains no proof of the Trinity – that you've been lied to, you're deceived, that God is one not three. 'You think you know your faith,' they are implying, 'but we can show you that your Bible doesn't even uphold your own beliefs.'

We have to be wise. We know that the Bible doesn't contain the word 'Trinity' but that this is a word which Christians down the ages have used to describe the beautiful and perfect relationship between God the Father, Jesus the Son and God the Holy Spirit, all of whom are fully God. So, understand where Christianity is coming from. Be confident in taking the Bible as a whole to tell the glorious story of Jesus and God's redemption of mankind. Don't get sucked in to trying to justify your beliefs with single sentences, isolated verses, or by responding to a specific challenge that is being thrown down for you.

Many times, I've been challenged in conversation with a Muslim to prove from the Bible that Jesus is God. I will start explaining that one of the main ways Jesus shows he is God is by using the phrase 'I am', which is the Hebrew expression for the God of the Old Testament, from when he first revealed himself to Moses. But as soon as I start explaining that path, they will say, 'No, I want Jesus' exact words. Tell me exactly where Jesus said that he was God.'

But Jesus did not stand up in front of everyone and dictate exact words. That was not his way. That question is using a Muslim mindset to try to disprove Christianity. The whole way Jesus communicated was to make people think. He spoke through his actions as well as his words, and he made things relevant to the culture of the time. He was constantly inviting people to experience and understand the mystery of his incarnation. So, you have the breakthrough moment, when the disciple Peter declares, 'You are the Christ, the Son of the living God' (Matt. 16:16, NKJV) and Jesus doesn't say, 'Yes, that's exactly what I said!' Rather, he says, 'This was revealed to you from heaven.'

When a Muslim says something like, 'Tell me where Jesus says, "I'm God, worship me,"' that has the potential to create a moment where you feel silly, you don't know what to say, and you wonder whether you really know your Scriptures. However, those who really know the Scriptures know that throughout his ministry, in so many different ways, Jesus told people and showed people that he is God. He revealed it by using Jewish terms and Jewish understanding of who God is – things that made sense in those days to people who did or didn't read, to scholars and shepherds and beggars and prostitutes. Not just to clever academics.

Don't let yourself be tripped up by the arguments that have been specifically prepared. Know your own Scriptures, and keep coming back to the basic fundamentals of Christ crucified.

The reason we get to talk to so many Muslims is that we do a lot of sessions in prison gyms. Some of the events we do in prisons are in the chapel, in which case I'm talking to people who have signed up for that, and often they are Christian, or already interested in Christianity. But we also do a lot of gym sessions. Sometimes we'll spend the day in a prison, and we'll do a few meetings in the chapel and a few meetings in the gym. Lots of the guys who come to the gym sessions to hear about the weights and the powerlifting will be Muslim, and they will of course also hear a little bit about our faith. In a gym session with, say, 100 men in it, I can get anything from two to fifty Muslims.

We handle a gym session differently to a session in the chapel. A gym session will be a bit more seminar-based. We'll be talking more technically about anabolic steroids, muscle fibres breaking down, how to do a squat, a bench press – things we wouldn't go into in a chapel service. But we'll always give testimony and talk about God as well.

I remember one time I was in a prison gym and I was warming up to do a Tough Talk presentation. The prisoners started coming in, and one man straight away walked up to me, put his arm forward to shake my hand, and really eyeballed me. He looked straight into my eyes, like deep in my soul to intimidate me, and said, 'So, you're a Christian, are you?' And almost with a mocking grin, he said, 'So you believe the Bible is God's Word, do you? But you know it's been corrupted?'

I knew exactly what was going on. How Christians and Muslims view their holy Scriptures is different, even though we both hold our Scriptures to be central to our faith. Muslims have a dilemma. If the Bible is true, then Islam is false. But they can't disregard our Bible, because the Quran references Christians[6] and Islam teaches that Mohammed himself is mentioned in our Scriptures.[7] So, Muslims believe their scriptures to be infallible, but regard the Bible as corrupted.

When a Muslim says, 'Your Bible's corrupted,' what they mean is, 'You have different variants, different translations.' Even the things Jesus said, and the message the apostles preached – they were spoken before they were written down – and that for them means it is corrupted. For us, it's nothing of the kind. The Bible is God's Word, breathed through humans, and as Paul says, it is 'useful for teaching, rebuking, correcting and training in righteousness, so that the servant of God may be thoroughly equipped for every good work' (2 Tim. 3:16–17, NIV). We engage our brains when we are reading and studying the Scriptures, and we ask the Holy Spirit to help us understand and apply the Bible.

We believe the Bible to be the Word of God. We believe it was inspired by the Holy Spirit, and written down by men. Some of it is historical account, some is poetry or song lyrics, some is in the form of letters to various people or groups of people, some is recorded conversation. All of it was written in a particular place and time.

When Job's friends are talking to Job, in the Old Testament, and the Bible records what the different friends are saying about his suffering, that's not God speaking at that point, it's Job's friends, with their differing perspectives – and we understand that. Not every word of the Bible is God's direct word to everyone in every circumstance. When we study the Scriptures, we understand context, style, purpose, direction.

With the Quran, every word is Allah. It's an eternal tablet. They believe it was already written and existent in heaven, and then through the angel Gabriel it was given to Mohammed. So, it is actually more untouchable than our Bible.

Sometimes, a Muslim guy has looked at my Bible, and said, 'What translation is that?' but he doesn't really want to know. He wants to get me into this argument about the corrupted Bible. We need to be really confident about our Scriptures not being corrupt. Because they're not. There are variants and translations – but the point of the Bible is the message of the Bible, which is a message you can put your trust in. The message is that Jesus is the Word of God. He really is the Son of God, he really did die, he really did rise again and he did it to take away our sins.

So, when this guy came up to me in the prison gym, and asked me about my Scriptures, I did not get into which translation I was using, or try to prove that the Bible wasn't corrupted, or anything like that. That would be fighting a losing battle. I just looked him in the eye and said, 'I have full confidence that this is the Word of God, and I trust in God's Word, and Jesus Christ *is* the Word.'

It's a spiritual battle. I believe he wanted to unnerve me. It might look like a human academic discussion, but it's a spiritual battle. I'm certain of that.

I mean, if you're into your apologetics and you get into all this stuff and study it, and want to go in picking apart each other's arguments and defending them in detail, and all that, well, great. You can go down Speakers' Corner – I've got good friends who do some excellent work down there, discussing things with Muslim speakers in great detail. They are very well-informed and educated, and it's fascinating to hear them talk. You can do your own research on the internet about the *dawah* and the Muslim approach, if you want to. But what I'm really saying is, if you're basically an evangelist, or a parent who loves the Lord, sharing your faith at the school gate, or someone in the office, talking to a co-worker – it's all about having a bit of understanding and being wise. Really, I just want Christians to have open eyes. I want us to be confident in our faith and in Jesus, and prepared for how we might be questioned and challenged by someone with a Muslim faith, so that we can be effective for the Lord.

Keep reading your Bible, keep praying that the Holy Spirit will open your eyes. You can be confident when you are witnessing and sharing, because you are sharing the true God. It's not about trying to prove this or disprove that in order to satisfy someone else's way of thinking. If people are actually questioning and searching, then God will use your actions, your words and his Word to reveal himself to them.

I had a conversation with a Muslim convert in a prison chapel once. He was helping set up the benches, and I was there early to be ready for the meeting, so we actually had a load of time to talk. He was a British guy who had been a Christian when he was growing up, but hadn't taken his religion too seriously. When he went to prison, he met some Muslims, and left his Christianity for Islam. This is a very typical prison conversion story, it happens all the time. There is a massive number of people in the prisons who have converted to Islam from a Christian background. Prison is a very particular environment, where people can be vulnerable, and there is a real benefit to feeling like you're part of one of the biggest groups, or brotherhoods. You see people going to Friday prayers in a prison, there are around 100 or 150 men there, and they're all looking after each other. There's a strong sense of belonging.

So, I was chatting with this Muslim convert in the chapel, and we were talking about whether Jesus was God. He was making the same sort of statements I had heard before: 'Show me in the Bible where Jesus says he's God, and tells people to worship him.' Those trained in this kind or argument will quote Luke 18:19, where Jesus says, 'Why do you call me good? Only God is good' (ERV). They use it as 'proof' that Jesus is not God. Now, that could easily shake a Christian who is not grounded enough in their Bible. You hear that phrase – used out of context – and you think, 'Hang on, that seems to say the opposite of what I thought.' What you need to do is sit down and read the whole passage, and look at what is going on, who is there and what Jesus means with all the things he says in this passage. Because actually, it is very definitely Jesus affirming that he is God, in the way he uses questions and conversation. Jesus is showing this man what's important in life, he's inviting the man to follow him, and he's challenging him to give up his immense wealth in order to join the kingdom of God.[8] We also know that Jesus does call himself good.

He calls himself the good shepherd, in John 10:11–18, referencing the good shepherd from the Old Testament in Ezekiel 34. Jesus used questions and cultural or religious references all the time, to make people examine their own minds, and understand their own thoughts, and help them work out who he was.

As I talked with this guy, I picked up a Bible and was flicking through it. We'd been sharing with each other for about thirty or forty minutes, while he set up and I got ready, and I just sensed that I needed to read some Scripture. I flicked to John 1, and I remember I had my finger in there, when he suddenly said, 'In the beginning was the Word, and the Word was God, and the Word was with God.'

I was amazed. I said to him, 'Why would you quote that to me?'

'I don't know, really,' he said. 'That's the only scripture I remember, from when I was young.'

'But why would you quote that?' I asked him, and I quoted it back to him: 'In the beginning was the Word, and the Word was with God, and the Word was God. He was with God in the beginning' (John 1:1–2, NIV).

I challenged him – I said, 'That passage is telling me – and telling you – that Jesus is the Word, and that the Word was God. And it goes on to say, "The Word became flesh and made his dwelling among us"' (v. 14). I lifted my Bible up to show him where my finger was. 'And the funny thing is, I've literally just got my finger in that passage and I was about to read it to you.' I said to him, 'I believe God is Spirit, and the Holy Spirit prompted you to say that verse at the exact same moment I had my finger on the passage. What chance is there that I would be able to predict what was going to come out of your mouth? Out of all these passages and chapters and verses, I've got my finger on the very scripture that opens up the reality that Jesus is God, that Jesus is the Word, that he is the Triune God, one in essence and purpose. And you yourself have just quoted that verse to me.'

I looked back at his face, and he looked like someone who'd just been told that his house had burnt down. I said,

'You really need to analyse this, mate. You need to get back to the God you grew up with, to the understanding that this is the true God, because you've made a big mistake turning away from Jesus.'

That's how the conversation ended, because suddenly the prison staff came in, the prisoners started filing in and we started getting on with the meeting. But I know God used that moment.

The Bible says, 'The god of this age has blinded the minds of unbelievers' (2 Cor. 4:4, NIV). So, we need to know our Scripture, but we also need the Holy Spirit to open eyes, because we want more than winning arguments. We are soul winners. Jesus said, 'Follow Me, and I will make you fishers of men' (Matt. 4:19, NKJV).

Then Jesus said to his followers, 'And who do you say I am?'
Simon Peter answered, 'You are the Messiah, the Son of the living God.'
Jesus answered, 'You are blessed, Simon son of Jonah. No one taught you that. My Father in heaven showed you who I am.'

Matt. 16:15–17, ERV

Chapter Nineteen

Shouting, Screaming, Listening

> For God did not send His Son into the world to
> condemn the world, but that the world through
> Him might be saved.
>
> *John 3:17, NKJV*

Ian

A church invited us to do a street outreach with them, in Norwich, in 2023. It had been planned for some time, but at the last minute, they phoned us up and said, 'Look, we didn't realise but there's actually a Pride march on today. Do you still want to do the outreach?' We thought about it, but we said yes. The church guys were going anyway, so we went.

We had a briefing before we went out, which we often do anyway when we're working with a church – a bit of a chat and a bit of a pray. But this was different, because it also involved security. There was a pro-life group also going out with us, with a stand to educate people on the issues around abortion, and a couple of guys who were security trained were coming out, just in case anything happened.

We parked up and walked through the crowds with our kit. It was a colourful, crazy atmosphere. There were extraordinary costumes – some of them very skimpy, some of them very elaborate – and endless LGBT flags waving everywhere you looked.

I hadn't realised how many thousands of people would be there. Afterwards they said there were 10,000 people on the march. It was quite a middle-class crowd, I would say – people turning out, thinking, 'This is a worthy cause – let's get out and support these minorities.' And there were lots of families – ordinary people heading out with the kids to see the parade go past and have a fun day. But for the people at the centre of it, there was this fervency, this absolute conviction. It was like a new religion, not just ideology or politics, but going deeper than that; a real passion, spiritual.

The people from the church were walking in front of us towards the place we were going to set up. Some of them had hoodies that said 'Jesus loves you' on the back, and the reactions to that were unbelievable. People were giving the finger, spitting on the ground, shouting abuse just at the sight of a hoodie with the name of Jesus. There was an immense hostility before anyone even opened their mouth. The perception was that we were bringing a message that went against what these people believed. It was like part of their identity was to hate Christians.

The church had picked a spot in front of a bank, where the pavement was wide and we could stand with our backs to the buildings. There was a space in front of us, and beyond that was the road where the parade was going past.

To the side of us, the pro-life group started putting their posters up, and as soon as they did, it caused huge conflict. People began shouting and swearing at them, really going for it; there was a group of thirty or so young people doing their best to completely silence and eradicate them. For some reason, a couple of them had a huge pair of Y-fronts on poles – about 10ft wide – and they were using the giant Y-fronts to try to cover up all the pro-life posters. There was one woman who was roaring at a poster. She stood in front of it, giving out a full-throated, deafening roar. She went on and on and on. She was proper losing it.

We had a log with us that day, to do a log press. We got the log out the front – it's about 6ft long – and Arf and I stepped forward, and started our usual patter: 'How you doing, Norwich? Great to see you people out here today! We're Tough Talk – we're a Christian charity, and we're going to tell you our stories. We've also got this log here – we're going to have a bit of a fun competition to see who can lift this log . . . '

We had our *Rocky* music going on, and we were chatting about the log press and to be honest, I think it really confused people. We were clearly something different to the main parade, but we hadn't got up and laid into the LGBT ideology either. So, because it was neither cheering them on, nor shouting them down, people didn't know quite where to place us.

We quickly drew a crowd, and when we started inviting people to do the log press, we got quite a queue of blokes coming up to have a go. By this stage, there were a few people yelling at us as well, because we had spoken the name of Jesus in our introduction. We always say upfront what we're about. We don't draw people in with the weightlifting and then suddenly reveal our Christianity, as though we've tricked them into listening. That's not our way.

A few people were shouting, and there was loads of noise from the parade, but mainly, we had a crowd of friendly faces.

Arf and I were standing there with our microphones, the log was on the ground in front of us, there was a queue of guys standing ready to have a go and there was the crowd all around.

Into that scenario came two young women. They walked in, stood themselves in front of the log – between us and the crowd – and started kissing. I guess they were trying to offend us with their sexuality. They just stood there, kissing.

Street work has changed a lot over the years, but the one thing that hasn't changed is that it's always a spiritual battle. The enemy is set on distracting people, and coming against our plans to share the gospel. Sometimes he does that with a drunk person wandering in and interrupting things. Sometimes it's even a nice, well-meaning person who gets too excited with being in front of a crowd, and ends up detracting from our key message.

The name of Jesus always offends, but in the past, it was mainly polite apathy we were coming up against. If people didn't like it, they would walk on by. The worst kind of protest action used to be people very obviously sticking their fingers in their ears, and crossing to the other side of the road. Not any longer.

I would say in the last ten years, everything has changed. The way the spiritual battle is manifested on the streets is totally different. You're much more likely to get shouting and screaming – verbal aggression and abuse. That seems to be the way things are done in today's culture, and there is an inner anger in people that is very different to how things were twenty or thirty years ago.

It's one of the reasons street work is so exciting, to be honest. You have to make a split-second decision about how you will react to hostile behaviour. Sometimes I will make a comment to someone who's yelling at me, get them into a conversation. Other times, it's important to resist the urge to answer back – you just ignore the interruption and get on. You need to be in tune with the Holy Spirit, moment by moment.

That day in Norwich, there was no physical threat. Lots of screaming and shouting, and the two women kissing, but nobody threatening us physically. So, we ignored the kissing and the shouting, and got on with things. We did the log-press competition, and there were quite a few strong guys around that day, so it was a good one. We told our stories – Jesus Christ changed our lives. We gave the gospel – God so loved this world that he sent his Son to die for our sins. We wrapped up, gave out a load of books and took some pictures with the competition winners – all with two women kissing in the middle of the space! I think they got into the background of most of the winners' photos.

They ended up looking quite puzzled, though, because they could see that everyone was enjoying our presentation and listening happily, and our message had nothing in it that attacked the LGBT community. That's not why we were there. We were there to preach the gospel, and to present the message in a fun way, and that's what we did. People really enjoyed themselves with us that day.

There's no point, in my opinion, in attacking a group of people. Firstly, people don't see themselves as sinful, but more importantly, before God we are all sinners. All of us. It's something I say every single time I speak. We are all sinners before a Holy God. Full stop. So why would I change that because I'm in front of a different group of people?

Most people judge themselves to be good people, and not as bad as others. I've even stood in front of murderers who all have a good reason why it wasn't really their fault, and why someone else shouldn't have done what they did. But before God we have all sinned. This is an uncomfortable message. However, you can't come to God until you know you're a sinner. You don't go to a doctor unless you know you're sick. The Christian message is clear – 'there is none righteous, no, not one' (Rom. 3:10, NKJV).

We're not going to shrink back from the gospel of Jesus Christ – because 'it's the power of God to salvation' (Rom. 1:16, NKJV). The Bible itself says that the gospel is an offensive message.[1] It's offensive to any individual and any group, because it starts by saying we're all sinners, and it goes on to say we all need Jesus, and it claims that Jesus is the only way to be saved.[2] So there right away, people are going to find that offensive, because they don't want to acknowledge God, or they don't want to believe they need to be saved.

We've all gone away from God. The world is like a ship sinking, and we're all going down to hell. But there is one who is calling out to us, who is powerful to save, and that is the Lord Jesus Christ. Christianity seems to be under the cosh for having some different views to the LGBT community, and the whole subject is a minefield, even within the Christian world. But for me, standing there on the streets of Norwich, my main feeling was compassion for those people, because they seemed so lost, and they were so very angry. What's more, their anger was turning against us, who were bringing the message of Christ – which is a message of hope for every single person. The Bible says it's God's will that none should perish.[3] God wants everyone in his kingdom.

Personally, I believe the Scriptures, and I believe what Jesus said. I believe that God created male and female, and the man leaves his mother and father, and becomes one flesh with his wife.[4] The Bible tells us in Ephesians 5:22–32 that this is a spiritual matter, and that marriage reflects the relationship between Christ and the Church. However, I personally don't think I can expect someone who is not a Christian to do anything other than what they decide to do. It makes absolutely no sense for me to expect someone who doesn't believe in Christ to somehow make their lifestyle fit my theology. That is surely nonsense.

Arf and I testify all the time that our lives were awful, really wrong. Without God, we lived sinfully. When we came to God, we recognised our sin, and then God gave us the strength to start living differently. The faith in God – the experience of believing, and the knowledge of his love – come first. Only then do you start making changes in your lives and lifestyles, as you are enabled by the Holy Spirit.

Even if someone listened to you, and sinned less, but still didn't acknowledge Jesus as their Lord and Saviour, what have you gained? The soul is still lost for eternity.

Arthur

We didn't get into any of these issues on the day. We never want to get sidetracked – we just want to give testimony to God's saving grace in our lives, and share the gospel of Jesus Christ crucified – and that's what we did.

I did get a bit annoyed, though. At one stage, while I was giving my testimony, there was a young woman pretty much screaming in my face, and that upset me. There I was, a 72-year-old grandfather, a pensioner, trying to have my say, and here's a young girl thinking it's OK to scream in my face.

I do think it's a phenomenal change in how people think they can behave with each other in this country.

Ian

We try to bring the gospel from a positive place, not from a negative place. It was hard – they couldn't hear us because they were screaming, and they couldn't hear us because their hearts had already decided we were the enemy. Yet, despite the screaming and the shouting and the kissing in the foreground, a lot of people stuck around and had a good time. Real seeds were sown that day.

Afterwards, we were packing up the log and our speakers, and there were two old boys there, probably in their sixties. We got chatting, and they asked us, 'Why were they shouting all that abuse at you?'

I replied, 'They believe that we don't agree with their lifestyle.'

One of them said, 'I'm confused. I don't know what's happening to the world around us. You guys were just telling people about your lives, and about God in your lives, and their behaviour was appalling. They were shouting and spitting and throwing abuse at you two. I don't understand it.'

I said, 'Mate, that's just the world we're in now. The Christian message is that offensive to people. The name Jesus is that offensive.'

Arthur

The culture has changed massively, but there is a flip side, which is that a lot of people are searching. We hear a lot about spirituality on different levels and different issues. Whatever they might be getting into, the fact is, people are searching. But most of them aren't going to church to do it. So, it's important that we get out there and share our faith. David Beckham once said that he definitely wanted his son christened, but he didn't know into which religion.[5]

And that just made me think, 'Why hasn't anyone given him the gospel?' Jesus said, 'The harvest is plentiful but the workers are few' (Matt. 9:37, NIV).

That day in Norwich – and pretty much every time we do street work, in fact – people listen and people respond. There are people out there ready and waiting to hear about him.

Who's going to tell them?

Ian

Joe and I did a street outreach just before Christmas 2023 in a little shopping street in Waltham Abbey. While we were doing the weights and sharing our story, there was a group of teenage girls who sat down and were listening, very attentively – listening as though they'd never heard any of this stuff before – and, of course, it's quite possible that they hadn't. This is another significant difference to thirty years ago. Many people nowadays have literally never heard of Jesus Christ except as a swearword. They don't know the Christmas story. They don't know about Easter. They don't know the gospel.

Joe was giving his testimony. He was talking about coming out of witchcraft, about that being a sin before God, and how it led to darkness and anxiety. He explained how he came to faith in Jesus, and was changed. And even though it was cold and wintry, these girls were sitting on the pavement, listening open-eyed, hanging on every word of Joe's.

I said to them, 'Do you want to come have a go on the weights, girls?' and they shook their heads, but they listened all the way through.

This generation has largely been brought up to believe that there is no absolute truth. So, to hear people being certain about something must be surprising. There we are, with a message that says, 'Actually, you've been lied to, there is truth. Jesus really did live. He really did die on the cross, he really did come back to life, he really is alive right now, and he really can forgive your sins.'

They listened to the stories – to our individual truth, and then they listened to the gospel – the universal truth. They were really attentive, as though they were lost in the story.

God sent his Son into the world. He did not send him to judge the world guilty, but to save the world through him.

John 3:17, ERV

Chapter Twenty

Preach the Word! Stream the Word!

I charge you therefore before God and the Lord Jesus
Christ, who will judge the living and the dead at His
appearing and His kingdom: Preach the word! Be ready in
season and out of season. Convince, rebuke, exhort, with
all longsuffering and teaching.

2 Tim. 4:1–2, NKJV

Arthur

One of the biggest things that has changed over these thirty
years – very obviously – is the internet and social media. The
pandemic had a big hand in that.

We had always been into using every mode of communica-
tion to tell our stories and preach the gospel. Our first book
Tough Talk – my and Ian's testimonies – was published in
2000 and reissued in 2011.[1] Ian wrote his discipleship book,
Christ the Bodybuilder in 2004. I did another book in 2007
about my story, *The Power and the Glory*.[2] Our next Tough
Talk book – which included Joe's testimony and two other
team members' – was published in 2008.[3] If people come to

us after an outreach, and ask questions or ask for prayer, or say they have responded to the appeal, we will often give them a book. It's a way of continuing their thought process. You don't know which contact God is going to use to reach people, and you just want to hold out every opportunity.

Right in the early days, Ian made testimony tapes on cassettes, and copied them to give out at his events. Later on, we made DVDs of our stories, with different people's accounts of coming to faith. We used to sell them after events, and sometimes give them away in prisons. We did a little film as a promo to send round prisons that might want to invite us in.

Even the Tough Talk hoodies we wear – they just have the logo, the words 'Tough Talk' and a bar with weights on – sometimes they just draw someone's attention, and they will ask about it. When we explain what Tough Talk is, they might be interested and stay, or they might shrug and move on, but the point is, we've offered that opportunity. We just like to use any means, really, to spread the gospel of Jesus.

Although I, for one, was not a big fan of the internet.

Ian

It was Joe who started getting us into the live streaming. I think it was me and him in the van on a long journey home, and we were talking about some interesting theological issue, and Joe went, 'Why don't we stream ourselves?' He set his phone up in the Sat Nav holder, and pressed the button. We carried on chatting, but we were streaming it on Facebook.

So, really, this whole streaming thing came out of the fellowship that we have on the road. Joe and I were so many hours on the road, and we just started to get his phone out in the van and say, 'Let's do a live broadcast!' We'd be coming back from Wales or something, driving through the night, talking about prayer at 3 a.m. in the morning, and often there were just a couple of people watching us, but that's where it started. Then when lockdown hit, God really used that aspect in a way we hadn't foreseen.

'Friday Night Live' started in March 2020 and it's still going now. It evolved from our Tuesday night prayer meetings in Loughton. The Tuesday night prayer meeting went online because of lockdown. But we suddenly realised that it made so much sense. Arthur was in Cornwall, so he had only been coming to the prayer meeting if it fitted in with a mission or something. He was initially pretty resistant to the idea of having a prayer meeting on the internet, through our phones or computers. It sounded pretty bonkers to him, I think, but once he'd tried it a couple of times, he was won over. It dawned on him that suddenly he could come to all the prayer meetings without leaving home!

Joe was near Cambridge, rather than Essex, so it worked for him too. Carl Lee, who was a regular on Tuesday nights, had moved away as well – to Guernsey – but was still a trustee, so he could do it when it was online. Rob Oram was another key guy with us at that stage on Tuesdays. He was an ex-copper. He was working as a legal representative, but he went on to be ordained in the Church of England. We were part of that process with him – he used to chat through all sorts of things with us at those Tuesday prayer meetings, and he was great at all the theological stuff. Rob moved to Hereford shortly before the pandemic, so he too could join back in when we moved it online.

On a Tuesday, we would worship together and pray for each other, but we would also talk through Bible passages or issues from a biblical perspective. So, when we started up the Friday session in 2020, we took that mindset but made it relevant to current issues going on in the world around us, and what the Bible had to say about them. Rob fitted very naturally into that format – he enjoyed joining in, he's great at discussing things, and he brings a bit of credibility with the fact that he's an ordained minister.

So, we went from being a sporadic 'Joe and Ian on the road' to a regular Friday slot, and we called it 'Friday Night Live'. It's still going now, every Friday. The regular panel is usually three of us, out of Rob, Joe, Arthur and me, plus one guest. We will interview the guest about their faith, explore an issue from the Bible, chat about a hot topic, anything interesting that gives glory to God. I enjoy it, and there's something great about not having to travel – I'm still speaking to a decent number of people, but I don't go anywhere or spend any time getting there! I'm hanging out with the guys, we're talking good stuff, and we're talking about God with a load of people listening. What's not to love?

When the pandemic ended, there was no question of giving up on the 'Friday Night Live'. Even when the lockdowns ended, we were still getting between fifty to seventy people listening live, and a thousand or so views afterwards. We have some very faithful listeners and others who jump in and out.

So, it naturally progressed, and God has blessed it to the point where now, people are coming to faith from it. The other night I interviewed our mate Adam, who I baptised in the sea down in Brightlingsea. His faith journey started with a YouTube video we had posted, then continued through participation in 'Friday Night Live'. It was powerful stuff.

Since the pandemic, and since smartphones and TikTok and online everything, people have much shorter attention spans. We might not like it, but that is the reality.

When I think back over the years of Tough Talk, that is something that has really changed. At one stage, we were doing meetings that were two or three hours long! We had weights, but not only that, we had a boxing thing going on as well. At one stage, we did a load of presentations in a boxing ring. There would be a powerlifting presentation, then a boxing demonstration, then testimonies, and sometimes it felt like about two hours later, you finally got to preach the gospel! In those days, people had longer attention spans. All we had at home was three TV channels, and that was it. Now, we sometimes arrive somewhere and they say, 'You've got thirty minutes, lads,' and I'm like, 'Arf, you gotta talk a bit faster today, mate!'

We've got our Facebook page and we do all the YouTubes and everything. Nearly every event we do now, we will film some of it, or I'll get Arf or Joe to video me speaking about it, beforehand or afterwards, or I'll just record a little thought or a moment of gospel, and we'll whack it up online. We've got into that, and God uses it.

Arthur

We ran a Tough Talk Alpha course online during lockdown and we had loads of people join in, from all sorts of places all around the world. It got to the point where we had to break up into smaller groups for it to work, there were so many people. We had a number of people becoming Christians from that, and others who got a lot out of it even if they were Christians already.

I will freely admit that I am not at all at home with social media – phones and all that. I don't even know how to switch some of these things on – it's alien to me! The doctors tell me they're going to get me an app on my phone which will control one of the things they've put in my heart. Well, that scares me to death! I'll certainly make sure to keep the grandchildren away from my phone!

So, I was very, very adamant that I wasn't going to get involved in Zooming, or livestreaming either. I just didn't want it. But when I realised, actually, this is another step for Tough Talk, this is simply another way of getting out the good news, I kind of swallowed my pride. I started taking part in the online conversations. And now I'm very used to it. I love it, in fact.

As well as the Alpha course, we did 'Tough Talk Tuesday Testimonies' in lockdown, then 'Friday Night Live', where we talked about issues – the world, politics, theology – and we interviewed guests, all Christians. We've had an army general, the evangelist J.John, a TV gladiator, an ex-porn star, all talking about their faith in Jesus. We've talked about answered prayer, unanswered prayer, ghosts, the end times, the resurrection. All sorts!

Some of those people who listen on Fridays have never seen us lift a single weight, but they come because they want to listen. Some of them don't even know we do the weights. It's all about speaking God's Word and using the opportunities that he provides for you. Whether that's in person or virtual, it's his Word and his Holy Spirit that can reach inside people and change them.

Adam's story

I'm an electrician, and I live in Brightlingsea, on the Essex coast.

I basically didn't believe in anything and I didn't have a faith in any shape or form. I was almost an atheist, really. I didn't have an interest in God. I felt Christianity was a bit embarrassing, if anything. I certainly didn't want to be involved. My wife, Claire, became a Christian about twenty years ago and had been trying to convince me to believe. I hadn't taken kindly to it.

Claire had come across Tough Talk when Ian preached at the local church during lockdown. She said to me, 'Just watch Ian's testimony,' and stuck a laptop in front of me. I wasn't that interested, but it was YouTube, and it was only seven minutes long, so I thought I might as well watch it. Surprisingly, I found it quite intriguing.

I went on to watch a few more videos, and then I started to watch 'Friday Night Live', which is the livestream that Tough Talk present, where they have a discussion or an interview on a Friday evening. I watched those and my curiosity grew and grew to the point where I thought, 'Well, there must be something to this,' and I started visiting my local church with my wife. I found that very interesting, and I started thinking, 'There must be something out there.'

Via my church, I asked for a one-on-one session with Ian. I wanted to have a chat with him, explain where I was, where my mind was at and see where he would point me. He pointed me to the Gospels, specifically to Mark. He told me to go away, have a read and see what I thought. I carried on watching 'Friday Night Live', carried on going to church and started reading a Bible.

Things changed for me gradually, but there was a particular moment one day when I was driving to work, when I suddenly started to see things for what they really were. It may sound funny, but it was like scales falling from my eyes. Literally, the world was looking different for me. For the first time, I saw things for what they were – the green of the trees, the song of the birds, the sky and the sun and vivid colours. What I think is, for the first time in my life, I was able to take in beauty.

It was a gradual process. It took about a year from then to the point where I was thinking, 'Yes, I'm ready to make a decision.' It was one of the Friday night sessions – the one where Ace from *Gladiators* was on.

At the end of those sessions, Ian will always do what I call an 'altar call'. He will invite people to pray a prayer of faith along with him, and ask people to say on the chat if they have done that for the first time. And this time, it was me. I followed those words through and said, 'Yeah, actually, I do believe in this.'

I started to help out with the church. There's always a regatta in Brightlingsea in the summer, and I said I would help out with that, as the church runs some activities, and this time, they'd invited Tough Talk to come along.

I hadn't told anyone that I was looking into Christianity. None of my friends and none of my family.

Ian and Joe came down to the regatta with their weights, and gave testimony and the gospel. Then they and I got into a conversation about baptism. Ian said, 'Have you been baptised, mate?'

I said I hadn't. So they both said, 'Why not?' and I didn't really have an answer!

Ian said, 'Well let's get you baptised, then,' and in my mind, we were saying, 'Let's find a quiet part of the sea where there is nobody around, and quietly get baptised.' But the fact is, Ian, Joe and Arthur – well, they don't do a lot of things quietly. Next thing I knew, Ian was on the microphone telling the whole town in which I lived, 'Come down at 3 o'clock today, and see someone get baptised in the sea!' And it was one of those days in Brightlingsea where there's something going on at the seafront, so everyone does come down – everybody – it's a big thing, the regatta.

So, I started saying to my local church people, 'This isn't what I wanted. I wanted just a quiet baptism, just me and a couple of people – it's all getting really big.' Then I suddenly realised that this was actually a test from God. It was like God was asking me, 'Are you serious about this, or are you not? Are you prepared for being seen to believe?'

So I said to God, 'Alright. I'll do it your way.'

Next thing I knew, my mum and dad were walking down the beach towards me.

I hadn't even told my mum and dad that I was going to church, let alone that I'd become a Christian and was going to get dunked in the sea publicly to show my commitment. And here they were, seeing it with their own eyes, along with most of the population of Brightlingsea. The pressure was intense. But when we went into the sea, actually it was 100 per cent the right thing to do.

I think actually it had quietened down a bit by then. It was mid-afternoon. It was like God had said, 'I've tested you, we're going to do it no matter what, so I'm happy for it to be quieter.'

I was baptised in the July of 2022 in the sea in Brightlingsea by Joe and Ian. It was amazing. I remember me, Ian and Joe having a massive man-hug afterwards. The next day at church, Ian was there preaching and I gave my testimony, walking through how I had come to faith.

Ever since then, my faith has continued to grow. I made a decision to retrain as an electrician, and I'm setting up my own business doing that. I know it's the right thing to do, but I would never have had the courage to do that without knowing that God's behind me 100 per cent. Amazingly, I managed to work my way out of my old company with a redundancy package instead of just leaving.

I've also been to Kenya on a mission, spreading the word about Jesus with my local church. I never could have imagined I would do something like that. Telling other people about my faith makes it so real, and stronger. I got my redundancy package on 30 June, and I was booked to go to Kenya on 8 July 2023 – a year after my baptism.

Everything that has happened has really been God-led. And, of course, my wife is absolutely thrilled. I don't think it's always easy living as a Christian. At first, it's a bit like you open up the gates to this massive meadow. It's beautiful and vast, and you run in, and you're sort of running round, not knowing where to go, just loving it. But then you realise that everything you do is going to be hard, because people won't like you for being a Christian.

I suppose that used to be me. I always thought of church people as a bit wimpy, and well-to-do, so I was pretty shocked by Tough Talk. They were like me. They were manly. I like their sense of humour as well. They are serious about God, but they make a Friday enjoyable and fun.

I don't like things really longwinded, so when they pray, it's short prayers and to the point, and everything they talk about, it's to the point and that really engages me. If I have to listen to someone saying something over and over with loads of waffle, I just lose attention really quickly, it's just the way I am. That's what's drawn me to them, without a doubt.

If I hadn't seen Tough Talk – first on that YouTube video, then on the online meetings – I wouldn't be doing what I'm doing or believing what I'm believing. I see them as my Christian brothers, they're family. That's how I feel.

Before God and Jesus Christ, I give you a command. Christ Jesus is the one who will judge all people – those who are living and those who have died. He is coming again to rule in his kingdom. So I give you this command: Tell everyone God's message. Be ready at all times to do whatever is needed. Tell people what they need to do, tell them when they are doing wrong, and encourage them. Do this with great patience and careful teaching.

2 Tim. 4:1–2, ERV

Chapter Twenty-one

Beautiful Feet

How then shall they call on Him in whom they have not believed? And how shall they believe in Him of whom they have not heard? And how shall they hear without a preacher? And how shall they preach unless they are sent? As it is written:

'How beautiful are the feet of those who preach the gospel of peace,
Who bring glad tidings of good things!'

Rom. 10:14–15, NKJV

Ian

If I had a choice for my son or daughter either to go to a Christian conference for a week or to go on a mission trip, I would always say mission. I know both of these options are good ones. But with the mission, that person will come back built up, inspired, changed in a whole different way.

I'm not knocking the conferences. I've been to, and spoken at, many conferences where Christians get together, and

I love it. It's amazing to be with the body of believers, and build each other up. But when you get up, go out and start being a 'doer' of the Word, not just a 'hearer of the word' (Jas 1:22–25, NKJV), it's different. Especially a mission trip out of the UK. Anything that takes you out of your own culture and comfort gives you a new challenge and a new perspective.

The comfort we have here in our country makes us complacent. Think of places like Nigeria or Pakistan, where Christians are arrested, or kidnapped, or attacked – where churches are being burnt and people are in prison for their faith, and yet their faith is strong. We come back on a plane to our own comfortable, more privileged Christian reality, and it feels like the church is asleep! Compared to the church in India, or South Africa, it's asleep. It feels sometimes like it's a wishy-washy, sleepy, lethargic, do-goody church. Where's the passion?

When we go on a mission away from the UK – Moldova, France, Spain, wherever – we actually come back more excited, more challenged to do the things of God than when we left. I'd recommend it to anyone.

When you're on any mission together – whether it's in prisons abroad or on the streets back home – you're sharing the gospel all the time. You're explaining it, and you've got to be living it. You're in that spiritual battle. You're aware of the spiritual reality, you're reading your Bible more, you're praying and pressing in together, and it enriches your faith. It's like when Paul says to Philemon, 'I pray that your partnership with us in the faith may be effective in deepening your understanding of every good thing we share for the sake of Christ' (Phlm 1:6, NIV). The fact of being together communicating our faith, builds our faith.

Arthur

People often say to me, 'Oh, are you off out again? You only just got back from the last one!' But it's actually when I'm *not* out that I get exhausted. Yes, it can be tiring on the road, but it's when you're giving out that you receive so much back in the process.

People also say to me, 'Arthur, when you talk about Jesus, you come alive.' Well, of course I do. I get energised and encouraged and fulfilled when I'm out there speaking about Jesus, doing the work of my Father.

Ian

I don't know what perception people have of evangelists, but we are ordinary blokes. I've got my business, Joe works in the city, Arthur's a retired grandpa with a home gym in the garage. We're all working, and then we're all evangelising. I would like to break down people's thought processes of what an evangelist is. It's not a big mystery.

An evangelist is someone who believes in the God of the Bible, who is convinced that Jesus is Lord, and trusts the work of the cross – that Christ died for our sins. It's someone who the Holy Spirit uses to speak with authority, leading people to repent and turn to Jesus.

You don't have to have some immense spiritual experience of God calling you to be an evangelist. We know now that it's our calling, but we discovered it bit by bit. We started small. We worked hard and kept learning. We carried on. That's pretty much it.

We are not all called to be an evangelist, but all of us are called to evangelise. All of us who believe in Jesus Christ are called to speak about him. There's a church in Norwich that we work with regularly, and they go out on the streets every single week. Their pastor has a great understanding of the importance of evangelism. He's setting it up as a habit, a normal thing that everyone gets involved in. He does the preaching. Others might tell their stories or testimonies. Some people help set up, give out leaflets, or simply stand and form part of the audience, praying.

I would encourage every single Christian at some point to do a little bit out on the streets for Jesus. Get alongside someone who is preaching, hand out a leaflet. Give out mince pies at carol-singing. Maybe just stand around supportively, watching your church friends who are preaching on the street. Whatever. It doesn't matter which role you play, but get out there! Do it!

My best advice to people who want to know how to start evangelising is this: Start. Speak honestly to people you know about your faith and your beliefs. Start where you are. Keep reading the Bible. Keep praying. Keep hanging out with other Christians. Then your faith becomes stronger, and you have a solid base to speak from.

Be alert for opportunities. Start by telling your story – how you came to faith, and what difference it's made – whatever your own story is. Be real. If you haven't got a dramatic conversion like we had, that's absolutely fine. Every conversion is dramatic, actually, because it involves a sinner repenting, and moving into the kingdom of light. If you have made a decision for Christ, there's going to be a reason for that, there's going to be a story behind it.

Arthur

When I'm out with Tough Talk and giving my testimony, I will often say to people, 'You can believe what you like. You can disagree with me if you want. That's not my business. But you can't deny the truth of my own testimony. You can't take away what I know has happened in me.'

That's the power of testimony. It's your own, personal story. People can't disagree with it.

Ian

It's about having the confidence that we have a testimony of Christ in our lives. Some people forget that God genuinely did something incredibly transformative in their lives, because it has become the norm.

Also, it's about having the childlike confidence that the Holy Spirit will lead us. Even a great testimony without the Holy Spirit means absolutely nothing. It's just a story. When you ask the Holy Spirit to be with you, then the words are going to land in people's hearts; people are going to find something that rings true for them. It's the Holy Spirit who makes the difference – not how sensational your story is.

Arthur

Originally I spoke a lot about what had gone on in my life – lots of violence, lots of drugs, the extra-marital affair – to emphasise what a 'Damascus road'[1] experience I'd had; what a complete mess I'd been in, and then how I'd met God. And originally, I probably left it there. It was like, 'I was a horrible bloke. I did this, I did that, I did the other, I found Jesus, hallelujah!' and that was the end.

That might be entertaining, but of itself it's not going to change anyone's life. People need to know that this joy is also available for them.

What I've observed in Ian is that he's grown as a man, and matured in the Scriptures; he has moved us on from where we were concentrating more on the testimony to where we are now, focusing on the truth of the gospel. That's the main change, I think, for both of us. The testimony is still important, but the main point of the testimony is to lead into the gospel.

Ian

We in Tough Talk have dramatic stories of becoming Christians. There's the violence, the lawlessness, the nonsense and everything, and then there's this extraordinary peace that we all felt. We all experienced that. But if you stop at the experience, what does that mean? Nothing. You've got to understand – and then be able to communicate – the reason for the hope you have.[2]

You have to intellectually understand the experience of being convicted of sin, the decision to repent . . . the understanding of how Jesus' death made the way to forgive you and free you. When you understand what happened on the spiritual level, and explain it to others, that is called preaching the gospel.

Yes, there was an amazing moment when the Holy Spirit touched us, but what happened then was, we looked into Christianity. We followed up that experience by going to church, asking questions, reading the Bible, weighing it up, and then making a decision – a conscious, intellectual, reasoned decision – to follow Christ.

Now, I really believe that the way the Lord gave us the name 'Tough Talk' is significant here, too, because it's not about the weights, or power or strength, it's about the talk – the tough talk – the message – the gospel. If it was me at that point all those years ago, I would've chosen a name that had to do with the lifting. I would have picked 'Team Extreme' or something. The ex-doormen were saying one thing, and the bodybuilders were saying another thing, but all of them were about the strength, the power, the toughness – nothing about the talk.

So, the fact that 'Tough Talk' has endured for so long as a brand is that as we've evolved out of that more hardcore lifting weights thing into preaching the gospel more, and discussing theological issues, the name has remained relevant.

People see us on a Friday online, or preaching in a church, and they will immediately think that we're called Tough Talk because we're prepared to talk about tough issues. If we were 'The Power Team' or 'God's Gladiators' or something, it wouldn't work.

Arthur

It's the reason we changed our website recently. Before, when you opened up our website, it used to say: 'Ex-hardmen from the East End of London! Ex-drug addicts!' and all that stuff. Now it says, 'Tough Talk are evangelists, preachers, motivational speakers and authors'.[3]

We are evangelists. I like to think we're motivational. Ian, I think, can preach the gospel as well as anyone else I've heard in the last thirty years. And with the help of publishers and co-writers, we've written a few books. That's who we are these days.

We'll always have our pasts, and we will always have that original testimony of what God did in our lives, but it would be strange to make that the biggest thing now. The last thing we want is to be three old blokes carping on about what we used to be back in the day.

Ian

My old friend Mad Dog came to see me, right back at the beginning, and I told him, 'I've become a Christian.'

He was totally disinterested: 'Yeah, yeah, Ian, I've heard it all before. You were bad and now you've become good. Great. Good for you, fella. I'm not interested.'

And I remember thinking, 'Why didn't that impact him?'

Well, that didn't impact him because that in itself is uninteresting, meaningless and irrelevant. What's the purpose of that story, unless my life and the *ongoing* testimony of my life shows him Christ crucified? Everything is a gateway to Christ crucified – that becomes the reason for sharing.

What's the purpose of something changing in my life, unless it leads to a larger, universal truth – which is, Jesus really did rise from the grave? Otherwise, you might as well be talking about a new high-protein diet, or a 'secrets of success' seminar with a motivational speaker, or a new pyramid scheme that's going to change your life. That's the danger if you just rely on the testimony and don't let the testimony lead to the gospel.

You need them both, and they will make most sense together, but the gospel is the ultimate.

Arthur

We've said it before, but we'll say it again. We are 'not ashamed of the gospel . . . for it is the power of God to salvation for everyone who believes' (Rom. 1:16, NKJV).

We do not hold back from talking about repentance, or about eternal judgement. That sometimes sets us apart from other speakers, or even other evangelists, but without those things, your gospel is a false one, or at least, it's incomplete.

We went to a Christian festival and did our presentation, and afterwards, someone said to us, 'You were the only people here who talked about repentance.'

Well, that's shocking, really. Firstly, people who have not yet come to Christ need to know that confessing their sins and turning to him is the first step. Secondly, if you're a Christian, you're going to be repenting regularly. It's not like you do it once, and then it's done. No. Philippians says, 'Work out your own salvation with fear and trembling' (Phil. 2:12, NKJV). And in 2 Corinthians, Paul warns us against getting complacent: 'Examine yourselves *as to* whether you are in the faith' (2 Cor. 13:5, NKJV).

You keep examining your life, and you keep bringing up to God the things you realise you've messed up. Otherwise, how can you stay close to him?

Ian

We did a Christian Fun Day once. We were invited to speak by the Christian organisation that was running it. There was a bouncy castle, all sorts of activities and stalls, ice creams and stuff. And we did the weights, our testimonies and the gospel.

And someone said, 'Why were Tough Talk talking about hell, on a Fun Day?' Well, I'll tell you why – because you need to hear about hell. Hell is not a fun place to be, and we'd like it if no one ever went there.

Now of course, if Arf and I started a presentation by saying, 'There's a heaven and hell, and if you don't submit to Jesus, you're going to hell,' then we'd be out on our ears and never invited back. But when we spend time sharing our stories first, letting people get to know us and where we've come from, show that we can have a laugh and relate to people, and then we say, 'Do you know what, we believe there is a God who will eventually judge us, and that we all need to settle things with him,' – well, suddenly people are lapping it up.

Sometimes it's worth having a little bit of indirectness. I give that story of Tony in my testimony, and I often say,

'I went into this church and met this guy Tony, and he said to me, "Ian, God is a Spirit, the Spirit of God has touched you, but you've got to repent. You've got to turn from all that violence, turn away from that life, you've got to get yourself right with God."'

So, I'm saying what I want to say, but I'm doing it as a story, in indirect speech – I'm having this guy Tony say it to me (which he did), rather than me saying it straight out. It's exactly the same words. You're just showing it to people, rather than ramming it in their face. That can be really helpful.

Arthur

The Bible says in Luke: 'There is joy in the presence of the angels of God over one sinner who repents' (Luke 15:10, NKJV).

The core business of God is saving people and bringing them into his kingdom. There is nothing more important. It's the reason Jesus came to earth, the reason he died and rose again. That's why the Bible says, 'How beautiful upon the mountains are the feet of him who brings good news' (Isa. 52:7, NKJV). In fact, it says that twice – once in Isaiah, in the Old Testament, and again in Romans 10:15, in the New Testament.

Sometimes people feel like evangelism is something Christians are supposed to do, and that no one will ever want to hear about it. Nonsense. For those who God is calling, who are at the end of their tether and realising their sin, who are starting to realise that they need something beyond themselves, there is nothing more wonderful than someone coming along and explaining to them that what they are looking for is Jesus.

Ian

So, tell your story, but don't stop there. Your story is vital, but it's not the whole story. It's not even the most important story. The most important story is this – that God loved human beings so much that he agreed to let his only Son come down to earth to reconcile us by becoming sin in our place, and taking our punishment in order to set us free.

He died, but death could not hold onto him.[4] He escaped the darkness, came back to life, appeared to many people on earth and then went back to heaven. One day – the Bible says this clearly – he will come again, and he will 'judge the living and the dead' (1 Pet. 4:5, NIV). We need to think about that, and we need to get other people thinking about it. Where will you stand when Jesus comes back? Because God has made a way, but you have to choose to walk in it.

Chris's story (Part two)

Things didn't change that dramatically or quickly for me when I became a Christian. I carried on training, and I carried on taking steroids, but also we started going to church. I felt very out of place there.

The Holy Spirit was working in me. I started to realise that I was full of anger. That was, in fact, one of the things that was motivating my training – getting out my anger.

I was struggling, to be honest. I had stuff going on with my ex-wife and our children – we were going through court, which was extremely upsetting and stressful.

I spoke to the pastor, and he recommended a course introducing Christianity. It was useful in understanding my faith better. He linked me up with a guy in the church, too, but this guy wasn't really on my wavelength. He had had a Christian upbringing, so he didn't really relate to where I had come from, why I took steroids, my perception of myself or my anger issues.

Then we were doing an outreach with the church, and Tough Talk were invited. It was Ian and Simon. They put on the bench-press competition. I chatted with them both afterwards, and told them I'd become a Christian off the back of their DVD. I asked Ian, 'How do you go to church with what you're doing, with the sort of bloke you are? They're all different to me, there's no men like me at church.'

Ian said, 'Why don't you come to our prayer meeting on Tuesday evenings?'

I did, and it made a massive difference. It was men like me, and you could talk about anything. You could talk about your problems, about sex, about men's issues, and you were in a safe place, you knew it wouldn't go any further, and these guys just got it, and lots of them understood the kind of man I was. And we all prayed for each other. That was quite an amazing experience, proper men putting their hands on each other's shoulders and praying for each other.

Church became different, then. I didn't feel so lost, because I also had the prayer meeting to go to, where I got what I needed under the skin.

Arthur came along sometimes. We were chatting one time, and I told him that I was struggling to train – my regular gym was too far away. He recommended a gym in Barnet, and Joe put together a training programme for me, for powerlifting, which I really enjoyed.

I started going around and doing some bits and pieces with Ian. Ian sometimes threw me in the deep end. The first time I went out, it was a men's breakfast in Enfield. Ian had said, 'I'm doing a preach, so why don't you just come for a bit of breakfast?'

I said, 'Yes.'

I went for the breakfast, and when I arrived there, Ian said, 'Oh, and by the way, you're speaking as well.'

I gave my testimony and I felt like a complete blabbering idiot, to be honest. But I did it.

The next time, it was a Pentecost weekend outreach in Leicester Square. Ian said, 'Bring your stuff, and you can do some squatting.' But when it came to it, Ian had brought an-other guy along who never did any speaking. So this other guy was down to do the squatting, and Ian said, 'You can give your testimony, then, Chris.'

There were hundreds of people there, absolutely hundreds. It did not go well. I tried telling a joke and it was a proper tumbleweed moment. It fell so flat that everything was silent, except for one homeless guy who started laughing his head off at me. But I didn't quit. I gave my testimony. I told them what God had done for me and how my life had changed.

It didn't put me off. I started getting more confident in speaking. I always wanted to go and just lift the weights, really, but I did speak quite often as well. We did a little rota of outreaches and I signed up when I could. I did quite a lot with Simon and Joe. I was still training with Joe as well, getting stronger, and this time, it wasn't out of a sense of needing to change myself, it was because I enjoyed it.

I did Notting Hill Carnival with Kensington Temple about three times – the same place where I'd seen Tough Talk for the first time. It was surprisingly different being on that side of things. I hadn't realised how intense it was. I would do some lifting, they would speak for a few minutes, then I would lift again, with a few more weights, then they would continue the testimony, flicking back from one to the other, to keep people's interest up. It was exciting and demanding. I would do three lots of lifting, increasing the weight each time, per session, and we did about five sessions during the day. I was done in by the end of it. But I loved it.

I went into quite a few prisons with Ian when I was available. If you were wearing a suit and carrying a briefcase it wouldn't work. But going in with the weights, that is the key, the opening. Those first reps aren't impressive, with just a couple of plates on, but it starts drawing their attention. Then after the first bit of testimony, you slot some more weight on. Then after the next bit, you go up again, until you're squatting 200kg or so, and that's impressive. Once you do that in front of them, you've really got their attention.

Now we're in a church in Cuffley, Hertfordshire, called Life Church. My wife went first, because Ian was preaching. I went a few months later, and chatted to the pastor, who's an ex-army Irishman who's really into his boxing. He's easy to chat to, and open to anything.

I said, 'What about a men's breakfast?'

And he was like, 'Yeah, organise it, get on with it, I'm up for that.'

So, I organised a breakfast, and I got one of the guys who used to work with Tough Talk to come along and do a chat, then a couple of fellas from my old gym, and another friend came along and then ended up joining the church as well. So, we're settled there now. It's a good place.

I didn't stop the steroid use immediately when I became a Christian. I carried on with those for probably about six months, but then it just didn't feel right. I was injecting myself. I remember loading one up ready to go, and then thinking, 'I don't know why I'm doing this anymore.' I decided that was it and I stopped.

When you come off it, you do lose a little bit of muscle and strength, but not that much. It's mainly in your mind. Your mind is where it all happens. I was getting more confident by that stage, and Joe had helped me out with that programme of powerlifting. So, all that was really helping me. I felt like there was a purpose for lifting the weights. I was accepted – by God and by the people around me. My faith was real, and was making me want to tell people about God. I had all these blokes that I related to, sharing life and training, lifting and talking about our faith.

Who needs steroids when you've got all that?

But before people can pray to the Lord for help, they must believe in him. And before they can believe in the Lord, they must hear about him. And for anyone to hear about the Lord, someone must tell them. And before anyone can go and tell them, they must be sent. As the Scriptures say, 'How wonderful it is to see someone coming to tell good news!'

Rom. 10:14–15, ERV

Chapter Twenty-two

Success and Legacy

Thus says the LORD:

'Let not the wise man glory in his wisdom,
Let not the mighty man glory in his might,
Nor let the rich man glory in his riches;
But let him who glories glory in this,
That he understands and knows Me,
That I am the LORD,
exercising lovingkindness, judgment, and righteousness in
the earth.
For in these I delight,' says the LORD.

Jer. 9:23–24, NKJV

Arthur

I was writing our trustees report, and there was a question the
trustees asked us: 'How do you see the future?'

I wrote: 'We will keep doing what we're doing and what
we've always done – show up, do our thing, tell people about
Jesus. We will carry on boasting in the Lord, never in ourselves, and we'll keep doing it.'

We honestly don't think to ourselves, 'What is the future of Tough Talk?' We just think, 'Where next? Who else can we tell next about our amazing Jesus, who we love and who keeps us going?'

One of our favourite verses that we often quote is from Luke 9, when Jesus says, 'No one who puts a hand to the plough and looks back is fit for service in the kingdom of God' (Luke 9:62, NIV).

The way we see it, if God has given you a job to do, get on with that job. Don't go turning around, looking about at what everyone else is doing, wondering if something else might be more interesting, or more glamorous, or more lucrative. Just keep your hand on that plough, and keep going!

We still keep getting invited to speak, and we're still passionate about doing it. So, there's two reasons we carry on. Plus, we keep hearing about people whose lives have been affected by what we're doing. God still uses us to bring truth to people, and to extend his kingdom.

So, we carry on. Ploughing on. Praise God.

Ian

Over the years, people have sometimes tried to persuade us to put Tough Talk on a more official footing. We became a registered charity early on, and we operate under all the structures that entails. We have a Board of Trustees, financial oversight, and we need to do that, to be accountable. But we don't really want to get any more elaborate than that. I'd rather just get on with doing what we do.

I certainly don't want to start setting objectives or reporting on our performance statistics. Because you'll never be able to measure or count the results of Tough Talk's work.

Sure, you could count the people who put up their hands, or who come and tell us they have prayed a prayer. But what does that really tell you? I've long given up on the thought process that because someone's prayed a prayer of repentance that always means they've had a born-again experience that will last.

Maybe I felt a bit more like that thirty years ago. I remember being in Rikers Island prison in New York. The whole prison stood up when we asked who wanted to pray the prayer of salvation. I remember walking out thinking,

'The Lord saved everyone in there today!' But you've only got to look at the parable of the sower[1] to know that the first commitment someone makes is just the start. How deep the Word of God takes root in their lives and how long their journey lasts depend on many other things – the decisions they make, the people they spend time with, the temptations of the world around them.

If you think you can save everyone, you're very mistaken. If you think that someone raising their hand at the end of our meeting saves them, or even that praying the 'sinner's prayer' saves them, you need to look again at your Bible.

It's not like, 'We got fifteen hands in the air – count them up, tick them off – add that to the spreadsheet, Joe!'

We love seeing people make a decision for Christ. But actually, what you're looking for is not just that moment, but the fruit after it. You're looking for changed lives, renewed relationships, different priorities and attitudes in that person. You're really wanting to make disciples. That's what Jesus asked us to do: 'Go therefore and make disciples of all the nations, baptizing them in the name of the Father and of the Son and of the Holy Spirit, teaching them to observe all things that I have commanded you' (Matt. 28:19–20, NKJV).

We do even say very clearly sometimes, 'Look guys, this isn't Father Christmas in the sky. God is real, but you've got a choice to make. If you want to make a choice right now, that's great. But there will be more choices that come afterwards, and those choices you make at home – to read the Bible, to pray, to surrender your life to God's way; those choices you make when it's just you – they will be equally as important as the first time you stood up at the end of a Tough Talk presentation.'

The truth is, the kingdom of God can't be somehow proved by outward actions. It comes to people's hearts. Some people will respond very quickly the first time they hear the gospel. Others might listen, but it doesn't all sink in. Not straight away.

Yes, we see people repenting of their sins and turning to Christ. That is a massive privilege, and it's what we want – to see God adding to his kingdom. But there are also many, many times when our work inspires someone to take a small step towards faith. It might be going and reading the Bible for the first time, asking the prison chaplain some questions about faith, agreeing to go to church with a friend who has been asking them for ages. The small decisions are just as important. Sometimes they are the decisions that last, and get built on and added to.

We are part of the seed-sowing process. We can't stick around and water every single seed and watch it grow, and weed around it and everything else. That's not the nature of evangelism. We turn up, do our thing, get the seed planted and that's our job done, pretty much. We have to move on and leave those other responsibilities to other people – and to God. Our responsibility is to do what God has asked us to do – tell our testimony and preach his Word. Everything else is up to the church and him.

The best things happen when our frontline evangelism connects with a decent local church that has a heart for the lost. Nearly all our street outreach is done under the auspices of a local church, who will still be there when we've moved on. That's so important to us. As evangelists, we rock up, say our piece, then off we go again. We make an impact, and we inspire some people to make a decision. But the people who respond to our appeals – whether on the streets or elsewhere – desperately need picking up in a proper relationship to be taken on to the next phases of faith and character building. We can't do that ourselves.

I admire the people who get alongside these new Christians and give them high expectations, and lots of really healthy attention and care and teaching. I love that. That's what we all need.

Really, my own personal journey is that my faith really got grounded for the first time when I was listening to a testimony from a guy called Noel Fellowes.[2] I'd decided to follow Christ, and I'd started to attend a church in Canning Town. But I was struggling to understand the gospel. I didn't know the Bible, and what I listened to every Sunday didn't make any sense for me. Then Noel came in. He gave his testimony, and explained some of the basics of the gospel, and it started joining the dots. His testimony impacted me, and I started seeing that the Holy Spirit was part of the Trinity, that Jesus was incarnate – had become a real person, to die and forgive sins; I just started getting it. It started making sense. I remember thinking, 'This is so important, this message!' And of course, that's the message I've been preaching ever since.

You can't assess what happens when you sow the seed. You're preaching the Word, you're holding out the bread of life. What happens to that is up to that individual person and the Holy Spirit working in their life. How many hands go up, how many people cry, how many say the prayer – those can be indications of God at work, but they aren't measures of success.

Arthur

Some organisations can put more of a figure or number on what they do. Back at home, my church supports a lady who does some work with a charity out in Eastern Europe, and she did this brilliant thing to raise money for a building project where you could sponsor a brick, or a drainpipe, or a toilet seat. That really captured people's imagination, and she raised a good deal of money. But it also got me thinking about Tough Talk, and how we can't do that. We can't point to a building and say, 'We built that.' We can't say, 'We're going to fund a hospital wing, or sponsor a shipload of medical equipment.' And that makes it harder to ask for money – because there isn't some physical output to point to.

We've been there when charities or churches have been raising money for other projects. Occasionally, we've been asked to speak or present, without a fee, and someone has used our event to raise money for another cause entirely. That can sting a bit, to be honest.

I've seen people giving £200 or £300 at a time to a building project, and I've been left thinking, 'I've travelled up and down and round and round telling lost people the good news of Jesus, and I haven't got a tenner for it.' Yet I know that people are generous, because I see them giving, day in and day out. And surely winning souls for Christ – what we do – is the very nub of Christianity. Isn't it? So people must support what we do. Don't they?

I think Ian realised long before me that much of the church does not really see or value the work of evangelists.

The fact is, our work is invisible. We're under the radar. We're going where the need is, not where the audience are. You can't come and watch us in the high-security wing of the local prison, or at a drug rehab centre. You can't see the results. But God can.

Ian

I believe an evangelist has two roles – to reach the lost and to wake up the church. It's not like a lovely pastor who prays for you when you're down, cares about your tricky marriage, visits when you're sick. We're not those guys. We're saying, 'Wake up! Christ is coming back! Preach the gospel! Share your faith!' We're here to shake people out of their slumber.

In terms of legacy, I'm much more interested in inspiring people to share their faith and tell others about Jesus' love and the power of salvation than anything else. I'm not interested in somehow making sure Tough Talk as a brand or organisation or whatever carries on. I'm not bothered about that. I'm not going to be on my deathbed saying,

'If I just know there are guys out there in Tough Talk hoodies, I can go in peace!'

If us three can inspire someone to get up and evangelise, in their own way, in God's authority, then that's what we want.

So, how I see my role as an evangelist is like this:

- Am I introducing people to the possibility of recognising and following Jesus?
- Am I inspiring other Christians to speak about their faith, and to share the gospel?

I certainly don't need to inspire anyone to be a bodybuilder or a powerlifter. But I would love the church to hear when I say, 'Wake up! Heaven and hell are real! Jesus is coming back! Share your faith! Have passion! Have joy in it!'

If we inspire a few people to go out with passion and preach the gospel, that's a real legacy, that's what I really want.

Arthur

There's a young man down here in Cornwall. I just texted him to see if he'll speak at a men's breakfast for me. He texted me back, and said, 'I'd be more than happy to come and speak. Listening to you and Tough Talk was what inspired me to get up and share my faith.' Isn't that brilliant?

He's a very good speaker, actually. Probably better than me. He's great. That to me is a legacy. He's not running around in a Tough Talk T-shirt, but he's getting out and evangelising. That's exactly what we want.

When I pop my clogs, I know Ian's gonna go on until he pops his clogs, and then Joe will go on. Not as Tough Talk, necessarily, but he'll always share his faith. And there are a number of other guys we know who have been impacted by Tough Talk and have gone on to have their own ministry, which includes sharing the gospel. There will be still others that we don't know about.

We say it often, but that's because we mean it. It's a great privilege to stand in front of people and share the gospel. It's a privilege spiritually that Jesus has given us the chance to do that, and to speak some good into men's lives. Sometimes I sit on the train on the way home, and I can't believe what God has done through us.

Ian

I want to say to people, 'Evangelism is just using what's in your hand to communicate your story and the truth of Christ.' I want to warn them as well that there is a spiritual reality out there, where there are forces of darkness who don't want you to go out and preach. They don't want you to tell people they can be free. And especially, they don't want you to speak the name of Jesus. Because the name of Jesus is more powerful than any other name. Acts 4:12 says, 'Nor is there salvation in any other, for there is no other name under heaven given among men by which we must be saved' (NKJV).

I believe God has given Tough Talk the ability to speak, and the ability to shape our speaking for all sorts of different audiences, and to do so through his power alone, not our own. We do prisons, we do schools, we do youth groups. We're at men's events, we're at rehab centres, we go out on the streets.

Even with churches, we've done a whole range – Assemblies of God, Pentecostal, Catholic, Church of England, Baptist, everything – even some on the fringes of mainstream Christianity. The only thing we are interested in is Christ, and Christ crucified. If a church or a group believes that Jesus is Lord – the Son of God who died for our sins – who will come again in ultimate judgement, that's enough for us. If they are saying that, then who am I to say no? I'm up and out there and preaching the name of Jesus.

The most successful things have longevity. Look at Alpha – it's kept going on and on with its original vision and real consistency. The fruit that has come out of Alpha is amazing. It has been probably the most effective thing for evangelism in our lifetime. That heartbeat came from Holy Trinity Brompton, and they have committed and supported it for years and years. But they haven't made it a personal empire or just used it to build their own church – they've devolved it down to local churches. They've built the kingdom of God and reached the lost.

That's all we want to do. Preach the name of Jesus. Enable others to preach the name of Jesus. Let go, and let God do what he wants with us.

So, here's my advice. Don't become an evangelist because you're looking for glory, or money, or a comfortable lifestyle. Become an evangelist because you believe that God is the ultimate King of the universe, because you believe in heaven and hell, and because you want to join him in his battle to win souls.

You don't know what God's doing in people's lives when you get up to speak. There might be someone there who's never heard about Jesus being real, about him dying for them, about the blood of Jesus that cleanses us from sin. They might never have heard that he came back to life because death could not hold him.[3] They might not know that he will come again in ultimate judgement, and finally establish his kingdom over all things.

There might be someone at the end of their tether who is going to stop and listen to what God says through you.

There might be someone who God has brought very close to him, who is just waiting for the word that will bring them into the kingdom.

And God might be planning for that word to come through what you say.

Don't you want to be part of that?

This is what the LORD says:

'The wise must not brag about their wisdom.
The strong men must not brag about their strength.
The rich must not brag about their money.

But if someone wants to brag, then let them brag about this:

Let them brag that they learned to know me.
Let them brag that they understand that I am the LORD,
that I am kind and fair,
and that I do good things on earth.
I love this kind of bragging.'
This message is from the LORD.

Jer. 9:23–24, ERV

Chapter Twenty-three

The Choice

Behold, now is the accepted time; behold, now is the day
of salvation.

2 Cor. 6:2, NKJV

Arthur

I will never forget the peace that came over me that night at
Spitalfields Market, when I said to God, 'Come on then, sort
me out.'

I will also never forget Vin, the pastor who counselled me,
saying, 'Arthur, you need to choose.'

Ian

At the end of every meeting, we will always conclude with
some kind of opportunity for people to make a choice before
God. In a prison chapel, in a church or on the streets, it will be
a full-on appeal for those who want to commit themselves to
Christ that very day. I'll pray a prayer of repentance and salvation, and I'll invite people to pray along with me, line by line.

In a school or a prison gym, it will be a lot more subtle. We may well spend less time overall talking about God and faith, but we will always do it, and we will always make some kind of space for people to respond or consider what we have said.

Arthur

You've got to be appropriate to the circumstances. Sometimes you lay it on thick, other times you take a longer view. We did a mission in Liverpool once where we went to three or four schools during the day. We didn't give a direct appeal, but we did say, 'If you want to know more about God and about our faith, there's this event on at a youth club tonight down the road – come along.'

So that night at the youth event, we did our presentation, and this time, because it was in a church, it was clear what the deal was – people had chosen to come along. We gave an appeal for those who wanted to turn to Christ, and three or four young people put their hands up to say they wanted to do that. The youth leader was ecstatic about it!

Ian

When I give an appeal, I very much ask the Holy Spirit to guide me. I haven't got a script. I don't say the same words every time. But I do make sure I go through the main points, which to me are:

- There is an eternal consequence to our lives. One day we will stand before God and have to give an account of our actions.

- No one is righteous before a Holy God. Everyone has done wrong, and none of us meet God's standards.
- We are called to repentance, and God will forgive those who repent.
- Jesus died to forgive us, and promised to give the Holy Spirit to those who accept him as Lord and Saviour.

I always weave Scripture into it. I want people to know this isn't just Ian talking, it's the Word of God, it's the eternal truth of the Bible. As the writer of Hebrews says: 'The word of God is living and powerful, and sharper than any two-edged sword, piercing even to the division of soul and spirit, and of joints and marrow, and is a discerner of the thoughts and intents of the heart' (Heb. 4:12, NKJV).

Arthur

Ian will give the appeal as the conclusion of presenting the gospel. What would be the point of explaining to people the possibility of eternal life, and then not offering them the opportunity to take it up? He will say something like this:

> You've heard Joe, Arthur and me share our stories today, and you may be thinking what bad people we are. But actually before a Holy God, and before his standards, each and every one of us has fallen short. The Bible says, 'all have sinned and fall short of the glory of God' (Rom. 3:23, NIV). The Bible also says, 'There is a way that seems right to a man, but its end is the way of death' (Prov. 14:12, NKJV). Before a Holy God, we are all in trouble. We've all made mistakes, and if you died today and

were to stand before your Creator, there are things you've done and said that you'd be ashamed of.

The Bible says, 'the wages of sin is death, but the gift of God is eternal life' (Rom. 6:23, NIV); God so loved the world that he sent his only Son, Jesus Christ, into the world to die for our sins.[1] He is the perfect sacrifice, who took our shortcomings to the cross with him, and triumphed over them when God raised him from the dead.

You can get right with God. Now is the time – the Bible says, 'Behold . . . now is the day (2 Cor. 6:2, NKJV) – to get right with him.'

Ian

To be honest, I pray and I allow the Holy Spirit to lead me. I don't mean to sound very spiritual, but the fact is, I don't think about it, and it always flows.

I try to cover death, hell, consequences, judgement, the cross and eternal life in a nutshell. I like that Romans Road to salvation[2] – those passages are the ones I try to tick off in my mind, as I'm doing it. And then I say, 'There is good news. The Bible says if we confess with our mouth that Jesus is Lord, and believe in our heart that God raised him from the dead, we will be saved.[3]

Today is the day of salvation. So, if you want to respond to God now, pray this prayer:

> Heavenly Father, I thank you that you sent your Son, Jesus, who died upon the cross. Forgive me for the things I've done that were wrong. I repent and turn from my sins. Come into my heart by the power of your Holy Spirit, that I may be born again and one with you, my sins forgiven, in Jesus' name. Amen.

Arthur

It's a great joy and a privilege when people come up to you afterwards and say, 'I prayed the prayer.'

It's so humbling and so exciting. I like to think of the angels rejoicing up in heaven over that sinner who has repented.[4] Whether it's the first time they have responded to God, or whether they are recommitting themselves, we will always encourage them to read the Bible, to get connected with a church and to get themselves hanging out with Christian men and women who love the Lord. That's so important, to get into a place where you are understanding what you have started to decide – where you're encouraged and discipled, and people can explain the Bible to you.

Ian

Sometimes I will ask people to put their hand up – maybe while everyone's head is still bowed and eyes closed – because there's a power in acknowledging that they've made that decision, and it means I can quickly clock people and make sure they talk to someone afterwards about the decision they've made. I'll always say, 'If you prayed that prayer today, talk to someone. Tell the person you came with, or come and speak with us.'

We're always happy to pray with anyone who has made a commitment. We'll be hanging around afterwards – whether it's a chapel, a church, a street corner, whatever, we'll be there to pray for people who have just taken that step.

Some people will come to us and they are visibly moved, even sobbing. They have been moved emotionally in the realisation of their own sin, and they have been touched by the realisation of God's love for them.

There was a guy in a prison who told us he had prayed the prayer, and went back to his cell, and later during the night, he was awake, and really started to think about the things he'd done. He said there were tears in his eyes as he thought about Jesus dying on the cross for him. Some people say it's like a veil came off their eyes.[5] Some people say they had an incredible sensation of peace. It's never the same for two people.

Some people say the prayer and go away, and actually it doesn't start anything off. It's like the parable of the sower.[6] We sow the seeds, but the seeds can fall on dry ground, or be withered, or be choked by the weeds. But my own prayer is that people go on and follow the faith and become a confessor of Jesus Christ – a disciple. That's our prayer. It doesn't matter exactly how it happens, but that's what we are after – disciples of Jesus.

Arthur

If they say, 'I prayed the prayer,' we will always pray with them that the Lord would protect the seeds that have been sown, that this person would go on and have boldness to share Jesus, to be filled with the Spirit, and encourage them to join a good church, because a church now needs to bring that person to discipleship, to baptism and all that. If the event we're doing is in a church, we'll probably say, 'This looks like a good church to us – why don't you speak to the pastor, or find someone here to talk through your decision today?' In a prison, we say, 'Speak to the chaplain – tell him the decision you made today, and get him to help you study the Bible.' Because the thing is, we've done our bit now. Joe's dismantling the weights, we're packing the van and we'll be disappearing, but there's a process we leave behind that's for the church, the chaplain, the body of Christ, to bring that person to maturity in Christ Jesus.

So you speak to these people, and it's brilliant, God has moved. He is good, and he has done some work here in people's hearts – and by his grace, amazingly, we have been part of it. But then we have to move on and leave it all in his hands – and the hands of our brothers and sisters in Christ. We say our goodbyes, pack up, climb into the van. Ian gets into the driver's seat, I go in the passenger seat, Joe is usually squashed up in the back there, and off we go. And it's like, 'Right, lads, where we off to tomorra?'

I tell you that the 'right time' is now.
The 'day of salvation' is now.

2 Cor. 6:2, ERV

Oh, my brothers and sisters in Christ,
if sinners will be damned,
at least let them leap to hell over our bodies;
and if they will perish,
let them perish with our arms about their knees,
imploring them to stay,
and not madly to destroy themselves.
If hell must be filled, at least let it be filled
in the teeth of our exertions,
and let not one go there unwarned and unprayed for.

Charles Spurgeon, soul winner[7]

Acknowledgements

We want to say thanks to some of the key people who have supported us and the Tough Talk ministry over the last thirty years, whose names are not already in this book.

Thanks to the Tough Talk trustees Michael Steward, Steve Derbyshire and Carl Lee, who have worked hard to make the charity the best it can be, so that we can go out and preach the gospel effectively.

Thanks to all the churches we have worked with to lift the name of Jesus, and thanks especially to our church families at City Gates Church Ilford, Epping Forest Community Church and Baglan Community Church. You guys are brothers and sisters to us, and communities where we feel loved and at home.

Thank you to all the guys who have come and lifted, given testimony, or otherwise helped with Tough Talk presentations over the years. May God bless everything you're doing for him.

A thank you to Ben and Megan Collins of Magnify Foundation, for their financial support over many years. Also to Brian Souter of Souter Charitable Trust, who has helped support us financially for many years, making our prison and schools work possible.

Thank you to our families – wives, children, grandchildren – who love and support us in all the different things we do.

Thanks to all at Authentic Media, particularly Rachael and Donna who helped us bring the vision for this book to life. Authentic have been good to us over many years, supporting us in publishing a number of books and resources, including this one, and we are really grateful. Thanks also to Jude Simpson for the many hours on Zoom, and getting our words onto the page.

Almost last, but definitely not least, we know that there are many, many people who have supported Tough Talk prayerfully and financially over these thirty years – people who have prayed for us, supported our posts on social media, provided financially or practically for the ministry, recommended us to others, invited people to hear us, read our books, given our books to their friends, and much, much more. Bless you all. We are fellow-workers with you in God's fields.

Above all, thank you to Jesus Christ our Saviour, whose sacrifice bought our forgiveness, and whose loves sustains us every day. We are dedicated to YOUR service.

Arthur, Ian and Joe

Notes

Chapter One

[1] Bill Conti, Carol Connors, Ayn Robbins, 'Gonna Fly Now'. From the film *Rocky*, distributed by United Artists, 1976.

Chapter Two

[1] Ian McDowall, *Christ the Body Builder* (Milton Keynes: Authentic Media, 2004).

[2] Arthur White and Ian McDowall with Millie Murray, *Tough Talk: True Stories of East London Hard Men* (Milton Keynes: Authentic, 2000; 2011).

[3] https://www.pfscotland.org/ (accessed 24 June 2024).

[4] https://alpha.org.uk/ (accessed 24 June 2024).

Chapter Three

[1] Elim is a Pentecostal church network that started in the British Isles back in the early twentieth century, and began by booking venues and holding meetings to preach the gospel in the power of the Holy Spirit. www.elim.org.uk (accessed 26 June 2024).

[2] Ezek. 36:26, paraphrased.

[3] See John 3:16.

[4] Thank You Music, Ltd: Noel Richards. 1991. 'You Laid Aside Your Majesty.'

⁵ You can read more about Ian's story in *Tough Talk* by Arthur White and Ian McDowall with Millie Murray (Authentic Media, 2000 and 2011).

Chapter Four

¹ Dominic Muir is a UK-based evangelist and runs the organisation NowBelieve, a Christian missions charity. See www.nowbelieve.com (accessed 15 July 2024).
² Matt. 26:35.
³ Actor and martial artist.

Chapter Five

¹ 1 Cor. 12:8; 14:6.
² Paraphrased.

Chapter Six

¹ 'My Lighthouse' by Rend Collective. © 2013 Thankyou Music (admin. Capital CMG Publishing).

Chapter Seven

¹ The World Wide Message Tribe were a British Christian dance group whose aim was to convey the gospel to young people around the Greater Manchester area. They were part of the Christian charity, The Message Trust – you can search for them at music.youtube.com (accessed 26 June 2024).
² The Romans Road to salvation is a helpful way of telling the gospel of Jesus by using verses from the book of Romans in the Bible, to explain the concepts of sin, judgement, repentance, forgiveness and salvation.
³ Jesus In My Corner Ministry. See https://jesusinmycornerministry .wordpress.com/ (accessed 24 June 2024).

4   Andy Flute, *Jesus In My Corner* (London: Austin Macauley Publishers, 2019).

5   You can read Simon's testimony in Tough Talk and Millie Murray, *Tough Talk 2* (Milton Keynes: Authentic Media, 2008).

6   See https://newlifepublishing.co.uk/blogs/real-life/simon-pinchbeck -the-cop-who-became-a-crook (accessed 11 July 2024).

Chapter Eight

1   https://www.lcm.org.uk/ (accessed 24 June 2024).

2   Phil. 2:6–11, NIV.

3   Anna Bartlett Warner (1827–1915), 'Jesus Loves Me', https://www .hymnal.net/en/hymn/c/51 (accessed 24 June 2024).

4   You can find out more about Jumping Jacks Outreach on their Facebook page: https://www.facebook.com/login/?next=https% 3A%2F%2Fwww.facebook.com%2Fp%2FJumping-Jacks -Outreach-100064472718879%2F (accessed 15 July 2024).

5   Charles Hutchinson Gabriel (1856–1932), 'I Stand Amazed' (https://www.hymnal.net/en/hymn/h/290).

6   Horatio Gates Spafford (1828–88), 'It is Well', https://www .hymnal.net/en/hymn/h/341 (accessed 24 June 2024).

7   Carol Boberg (original: 'O Store Gud'), 'How Great Thou Art' (1859–1940), https://hymnary.org/text/o_lord_my_god_when_i_ in_awesome_wonder, translated by Stuart K. Hine (1899–1989) (accessed 24 June 2024).

8   1 Cor. 14:1–3.

9   https://www.tclondon.org.uk (accessed 24 June 2024).

10 https://www.draytonhall.org.uk/ (accessed 15 July 2024).

11 David Wilkerson, *The Cross and the Switchblade* (New York: Bernard Geis Associates, 1963).

Chapter Nine

1   Matt. 10:42.

Chapter Ten

1 Ezek. 36:26.
2 Martin Saunders, *East End to East Coast* (Milton Keynes: Authentic Media, 2002).
3 Luke 7:40–50.

Chapter Eleven

1 Prov. 26:11.

Chapter Twelve

1 John Newton (1726–1807), 'Amazing Grace!', https://hymnary.org/text/amazing_grace_how_sweet_the_sound (accessed 25 June 2024).
2 Matt. 22:32.
3 C.H. Spurgeon, *The Complete Works of C.H. Spurgeon, Volume 32, Sermons 1877 to 1937* (Morrisville, PA: Delmarva Publications, 2013).
4 See https://paulwasherquotes.wordpress.com/category/paul-washer-quotes/ (accessed 26 June 2024).
5 Luke 9:23, paraphrased.

Chapter Sixteen

1 Neh. 8:10.
2 https://www.bu.edu/missiology/missionary-biography/l-m/livingstone-david-1813-1873/ (accessed 15 July 2024).
3 https://ericliddell.org/about-eric-liddell/ (accessed 15 July 2024).
4 https://omf.org/about-us/our-story/ (accessed 15 July 2024).

Chapter Seventeen

1 1 Cor. 4:15.

Chapter Eighteen

1   The Quran references Jesus as *Kalimat Min Allah* (Word of God) in Sura 339 and 4.171.
2   The Quran references Jesus as *Ruh* (spirit) – in Sura 4.171.
3   In Sura 3 (*Al Imran*) and 19 (*Mariam*) the angel announces to Mary that she will bear Jesus even though she's a virgin.
4   Sura An-Nisa 171.
5   Sura An-Nisa 156–158.
6   Sura Al-Ma'idah-68.
7   https://en.wikipedia.org/wiki/Muhammad_and_the_Bible (accessed 1 August 2024). For discussions around this question, see https://aboutislam.net/counseling/ask-about-islam/prophet-muhammad-mentioned-bible/, https://islamqa.info/en/answers/44018/is-the-prophet-muhammad-peace-and-blessings-of-allaah-be-upon-him-mentioned-in-the-bible and https://www.alislam.org/articles/biblical-prophecies-about-muhammad/ (all accessed on 2 August 2024).
8   Luke 18:18–30.

Chapter Nineteen

1   1 Cor. 1:23; 2 Cor. 2:15–16.
2   Acts 4:12.
3   2 Pet. 3:9.
4   Matt. 19:4; Gen. 1:27; Mark 10:8.
5   https://www.irishexaminer.com/lifestyle/arid-30045061.html (accessed 1 August 2024).

Chapter Twenty

1   Arthur White, Ian McDowall with Millie Murray, *Tough Talk* (Milton Keynes: Authentic Media, 2000; 2011).
2   Arthur White and Martin Saunders, *The Power and the Glory* (Milton Keynes: Authentic Media, 2007).

3   Millie Murray, *Tough Talk 2* (Milton Keynes: Authentic Media, 2008).

Chapter Twenty-one

1   Acts 9.
2   1 Pet. 3:15.
3   https://www.tough-talk.com/ (accessed 26 June 2024).
4   Acts 2:24.

Chapter Twenty-two

1   See Matt. 13:1–9.
2   Noel Fellowes works for Christian Prison Ministries and is the author of the book, *Killing Time* (Oxford: Lion Books, 1996).
3   Acts 2:24.

Chapter Twenty-three

1   John 3:16, paraphrased.
2   Mentioned above in chapter seven.
3   Rom. 10:9.
4   Luke 15:7.
5   2 Cor. 3:16.
6   Matt. 13:1–23.
7   From Charles Spurgeon's sermon, 9 December 1860, from the Metropolitan Tabernacle Pulpit Volume 7 – see https://www.spurgeon.org/resource-library/sermons/the-wailing-of-risca/#flipbook/ (accessed 26 June 2024).

Authentic

We trust you enjoyed reading this book from Authentic. If you want to be informed of any new titles from this author and other releases you can sign up to the Authentic newsletter by scanning below:

Online:
authenticmedia.co.uk

Follow us: